LIGHT AS LIGH

Volume 93

Sun Tracks

An American Indian Literary Series

SERIES EDITOR

Ofelia Zepeda

EDITORIAL COMMITTEE

Larry Evers

Joy Harjo

Geary Hobson

N. Scott Momaday

Irvin Morris

Simon J. Ortiz

Craig Santos Perez

Kate Shanley

Leslie Marmon Silko

Luci Tapahonso

SIMON J. ORTIZ

LIGHT

AS

LIGHT

POEMS

THE UNIVERSITY OF
ARIZONA PRESS

TUCSON

The University of Arizona Press
www.uapress.arizona.edu

We respectfully acknowledge the University of Arizona is on the land and territories of Indigenous peoples. Today, Arizona is home to twenty-two federally recognized tribes, with Tucson being home to the O'odham and the Yaqui. Committed to diversity and inclusion, the University strives to build sustainable relationships with sovereign Native Nations and Indigenous communities through education offerings, partnerships, and community service.

ISBN-13: 978-0-8165-5025-8 (hardcover)
ISBN-13: 978-0-8165-5024-1 (paperback)
ISBN-13: 978-0-8165-5026-5 (ebook)

Cover design by Kevin Coochwytewa
Designed and typeset by Leigh McDonald in Bell MT Std and Brother 1816 (display)

Publication of this book is made possible in part by the proceeds of a permanent endowment created with the assistance of a Challenge Grant from the National Endowment for the Humanities, a federal agency.

Library of Congress Cataloging-in-Publication Data
Names: Ortiz, Simon J., 1941– author.
Title: Light as light : poems / Simon J. Ortiz.
Other titles: Sun tracks ; v. 93.
Description: Tucson : University of Arizona Press, 2023. | Series: Sun tracks: an American Indian literary series ; volume 93
Identifiers: LCCN 2022053751 (print) | LCCN 2022053752 (ebook) | ISBN 9780816550258 (hardcover) | ISBN 9780816550241 (paperback) | ISBN 9780816550265 (ebook)
Subjects: LCGFT: Poetry.
Classification: LCC PS3565.R77 L54 2023 (print) | LCC PS3565.R77 (ebook) | DDC 811/.54—dc23/eng/20230126
LC record available at https://lccn.loc.gov/2022053751
LC ebook record available at https://lccn.loc.gov/2022053752

Printed in the United States of America
♾ This paper meets the requirements of ANSI/NISO Z39.48-1992 (Permanence of Paper).

CONTENTS

Preface   *ix*

When I think of air pollution, I think of China.   3
i wake this morning at 4 am   4
A Sort of Poem or Sort of Story For Red Petal Girl   5
For Now   7
Ganges   8
How Did You Know I Would Be Here I Don't Know I Said I Just Did   9
Saying What You Have To   10
I Miss You Right This Minute. I Just Do.   11
Bone-deep Gladness: A Tiny Note From Red Petal Girl And My Own Notes   12
Not Too Soon A Poem Comes Like The Evening Star So Far Far Away   14
Looking toward the Sangre de Cristo Mountains across the valley, I can't see   15
Writing An Anti-war Poem, July 19, 2014   17
Already July 30, 2014?   18
When We Were Kids   21
Quails came by and made me smile.   22
Views From Shtaa'mah—My Home—Where I Grew Up   24
Tiny Tiny Heart Like A Seed   25
When You're Here In September Let's Find A Desert Spot   26
Just An Old Story You Might Know Already   27

Freedom And The Lie: Monticello And Thomas Jefferson And The Plan   28
I Don't Quite Know   29
Night Sky Dreaming All The Way Beyond The Milky Way   31
Giving Receiving Giving   32
With Love And Awe   33
Moon Croon by Red Boy   34
Forever is True?   35
Turns   36
Memory   37
Flying Red Petal Girl   38
Technology Trappings & Grandmother Spider   39
Always Memory. Jake, Me, You, Youth, and "A Chore and Task"   41
Crystal. Chrystals.   43
Language Dancing. Maybe.   44
That Girl   46
Fig   47
Hihdruutsi & Tuzigoot Rock Lizards Remember   48
What Is The Shape Of A Leaf?   49
Rex Barking At The Magpies   50
A Long Time Ago Story   51
Question Yes & No   52
Crickets   53
What If   54
Seven Tsinah   55
Tsunuunuu'gah   57
Beauty as Turquoise   58
Awake All Night   59
Prayer   60
Dreams and Reality   61
Arthur the Cat Staring With an Intense Meditative Gaze   62
Have You Ever Heard of a Horse Whisperer?   64
Salvation Or Else   67
Piccolo: Octave Higher Than the Ordinary Flute   70
Random   71
Grandfather and Granddaughter Listening and Hearing   72
All of These and More Love   73
Reminder   74

Jumping Beyond   75

Song   76

Flaring: Thought Into Color   78

Prayers for Raho   79

    Past   80

    Present   81

    Future   82

    Caring   83

How   84

Thunder Flower   85

A Poem That's Not A Poem But What It Is Only A Poem Can Say Words
    As Such Are A Poor Excuse For Anything But A Poem   86

O My   87

A New Dance Song For Thunder Woman Gentle and Strong   88

East Is Sunrise. And Then What?   89

Red Boy Thinks, You Think?   90

Going And Coming   92

Ode To A Tree, By Rb   94

Scares the Shit Out of Me   95

Awe: For Better or Worse   96

Kee Cumeh Sheh Dzah'dze Ha'maah De'ieu-nahmaa'tyuh. It Was Because
    One Never Appreciated It. Kee Guwaah Tsieu-peh-taanih?
    How did the story go?   97

I Was Thinking of Time   99

Building and Holding and Carrying   100

Love Poem Called Quite A Tasty Car, Yeah?   101

Wonder & Heaven/Hell   102

A Love Poem   103

Nest   105

Beautiful   106

Love   107

Guwaadzi, Amoo-uh   108

Repetition   109

Spoonful Can Have And Should Have Two L's?   110

Sharing. Breathing. Talking. Loving Yourself. Loving Others.   111

Flourish   112

Hi Jami Love,   113

Ever   114

Thank You   115

Letter From Indio   116

Years of Past, Present, Future. Memory. Toward Love.   117

Wanting and Needing   118

Hummingbird Humming   119

light strands between shells and cactus   120

Love Time Is Now And Not Too Soon Nor Too Late   121

Flowering   122

She Writes A Poem With Love. I Write A Poem With Love.   123

Looking Forward   124

Parent – Child – Reply   125

There And Ever: A China Moment   126

Qcui'skah Kahguutrutih, Amoo-uh Always   127

All Best, Simon J. Ortiz   128

Face Time Face   129

After my run this morning   130

Don't forget to look at the moon and the mountains.   131

Valentine's Day, February 2022, Love Is Still Love and More   132

Way To Go, Dylan   133

We Shall Endure   134

Casuse   135

Resistance   136

Marching: Being There Alive   137

Must   138

Clear Creek: A Favorite Love Poem?   139

Poetry Is Like This: Forever Life With Words   140

How And Why and Not Knowing   142

I Think You Would Have Loved Me When I Was A Boy   143

THE END   145

Acknowledgments   147

Notes   149

PREFACE

WORDS OF POETRY. Words as experiences. Thoughts and ideas as experiences. Actions as thoughts. Verbalization. That's what it comes down to. Words as action. Words in experience. Words with emotion. Too much thought is not what poetry needs. Thoughts-ideas in and of themselves are overrated sometimes. Don't forget words as emotion. Work it out. With poetry. And then you'll know.

Light As Light as a poetry collection is dedicated to my beloved Jami. Central to our relational dynamic, Jami and I email or text each other whenever we're not with each other: letters and notes, dialogues, and interchanges. These result in a dynamic of poetic lingo and expression. Many of my poems in this collection were written as a result within that dynamic. Her writing is included to a small extent and noted in footnotes. I am thankful to say Jami is inspirational and lovingly essential to my life and its realities and its meaningfulness.

I shall also mention her Acoma name, Qcui'skah Kahguutrutih, that I gave her: Purple Flower. My cultural heritage is Indigenous since I am a tribal member of Acoma. I'm a citizen of the Aacqumeh Nation and its people, who are formally included within the USA nation-state for better or worse. My first language is Keres, the original Indigenous language spoken by Aacqumeh hanoh. The name Qcui'skah Kahguutrutih is from that language. The Acoma people live in the state of New Mexico that is now known as part of the Southwestern USA.

Within the land area where I grew up, there's a landmark volcanic formation near an Aacqumeh village. Known as Flower Mountain—Kahguutratih Kuuti in the

Aacqumeh language—the landmark is near an I-40 turn off to ACL Hospital and Sky City Casino. It is called a mountain although actually it is a very tall hill. Once, driving on I-40 by Kahguutratih Kuuti, I told Jami that purple flowers grow on the volcanic hill. Purple flowers brightly fluttering in constant breezes. "Very pretty purple flowers. They always make me happy," I said. I've always felt happy seeing purple flowers because they are special to me.

It was at that moment, Jami said, "I want to be a purple flower." Later, some time afterward, I was joyfully singing a made-up ditty for her. The occasion? Well, after a long moment of loving, I was feeling giddy, happy, spontaneous, and, yes, a bit casual. The Keres words "Qcui'skah Kahguutrutih" came into the ditty. Poetic license? Well, it had to do with pretty purple flowers that grow atop and on the slopes of Kahguutratih Qcuuti. And I said with a big smile, "Why not then. From now on, you are Purple Flower. Qcui'skah Kahguutrutih." That's when Jami became Qcui'skah Kahguutrutih to me.

Poetry enhances life—your lives as human beings and my life as a human being—and life enhances poetry. Our sense and understanding of the world around us is a collaboration of understanding. Words and thoughts and emotions act-work together to provide and create meaning. And meaning comes from the collaboration or inter-action that takes place between us and the world we are a part of. Yes, that means we are with other living beings like birds, squirrels, dogs, cats, horses, and plants like sunflowers and spinach, trees, seaweed. Yes, all the myriad species and forms of life that are in the world; all life that exists in the world in fact. Yes, as people we are part of all volcanoes, oceans, deserts, tornados, and hurricanes, sands, stones, rivers, and lakes; yes, we are with all life and peoples of this world with their differing languages, behaviors, heartaches, joys, mysteries, cultures, histories, prejudices. They and we are the poetry that poetry is. My my oh my ai, my my oh mai aiii aii, mylai oh my aiiii. And that's what I am saying with my poetry in this book.

And I must never forget to say to my three loving children, Raho, Rainy, Sara and their children, that is, my grandchildren and great-grandchildren, and to my step-children Brian, Dylan, and Phil: I love you all. Remember that always: our love for all things and peoples is a must. Our love for everyone and everything. That's what makes poetry work. Shrai howbah ahmoo shrowaadrumah. All of you, I love. Ahmoo howbah aiii haah aiiii.

LIGHT AS LIGHT

When I think of air pollution, I think of China. It was even worse on my latest visit to China than it was last year, and in my visit before then in 2003 or 2004. I thought it was bad then.

This time I got back here to the U.S. with phlegm in my throat and chest. And I could not get rid of it practically for two or three weeks. And likely it came from the air pollution in China.

Is it like that all the time? Especially in Beijing and Xining.

I think of a conversation between Red Boy and Magpie. Between coughs.

> Coughs. Coughs some more. Coughs again.
> *Aaaargh.* Hacking a big one, a big gob, that is.
> *Hehhhhk.* Big gob spit, that's what Red Boy does.
> Now, ah now, I can breathe. Feels like air used to feel.
> Magpie, says Red Boy, you know that song?
> What song? says Magpie.
> That song you know.
> What song you know I know?
> Haarrraaika. That song. Haarraika.
> Oh yeah, the song. Haaaraaiiiika ah ahhhh.
> Yeah. Breathe, then spit. Breathe, then spit!
> Haaaraiiiika ah, haaaraiiikkkkaa, ah, ah, ahaaa . . .
> Red Boy coughs, coughs, coughs, Haaarrrai . . .
> Coughs again. . . . aaiiiieeeka. Ah ahaaaaa. Ha ha ha
> Rai rai aiieeeeh, *aaargh, hehkkk!!!* Breathingggg!
> We need good breathing air, Magpie, yes, good, good air.

i wake this morning at 4 am

i think it's too early

too early is better than too late though i think

okay

drive back to arizona in the dark

i will let the mountains and the valleys and early morning guide me

yes let them and let me guide me

too often i've questioned myself

this morning still dark i let me be my guide

soon the dawn be thankful for the dawn yes i tell myself

A SORT OF POEM OR A SORT OF STORY

FOR RED PETAL GIRL

dark early morn lasts only an hour or less

so by the time i get to deetseyamah where i was a boy

it is light and the sun follows right on my left shoulder

guiding me so i make sure i say thank you ooshrahtrah

passing by jumbles of rugged volcanic black rock

that are miles of jagged solidified lava dineh hanoh say

is yei monster's blood and the aacqumeh hanoh say is

tsemaashah a thick very sticky and gooey pine pitch

tsemaashah skquuyuh was cooking up to throw the hero boys into

but the boys shot blinding arrows into tsemaashah's eyes so

the skuuyuh monster kicked the boiling hot kettle of tsemaashah over

and it spilled for miles and miles and thousands upon thousands

of years so it's still there jaggy and dangerous and scary as ever

it makes sense doesn't it   as stories go i mean   i mean why not

i think of years and years ago and think of years and years later when red petal girl is flying continents and oceans ago to now

i think of her again just before i turn south at holbrook

when i see two tiny dinosaurs gracefully dancing and prancing

across the arizona desert prairie west of the painted desert

they're approaching i-40 and will leap over it like it isn't even there

and i think of me waiting for red petals to drift down gently from sky

ah yes it makes sense doesn't it thousand of years ago to now

FOR NOW

is everything beyond edgy
risk is risk is risk is risk sure
all but the smartest know that for now

tomorrow is tomorrow
the same way the era before now is
a common enough knowledge

for now for now and a day before
forever lesser or more sacred
a target locus we might figure out

take today or this evening or midnight
is it now yours or is it its own a day later
for now what to do but own it as ours for now

GANGES

is above

and below

and the future

and the past

in between

is here

but changing

into the moment

that is forever

we

know

time

again

and

again

I've never been there. But I've been there because the future is not yet now. And the past is past but evolving into then.
This perhaps is what Sylvia Plath came to know as now.

HOW DID YOU KNOW I WOULD BE HERE

I DON'T KNOW I SAID I JUST DID

tarmac

i stood there for a while waiting
2, 3, 4 jet passenger planes shuddering left to right

muted thunder becomes the skin
i wear staring eastward looking

another horizon another city elsewhere
i think of paris shanghai san francisco

where from here i ask myself again
i almost feel like hooking my thumb

upward rather sardonically hearing me
say: i hitchhiked from xining city china

some days ago a tarmac nothing but flat
2, 3, 4 passenger planes leaving caught the 8th one

tarmac fantasy makes me wish and long
to say: i don't know   i said   i just did

SAYING WHAT YOU HAVE TO

Saying what you have to.
Not saying what you don't have to.

Both ways are correct.
Do we have a choice?

Sometimes yes. Sometimes no.
Sometimes you go either way.

Doesn't sound like poetry.
So what do you do?

I answered a question a couple of days ago.
Is English useful to you as an Indigenous person?

No, I said. Sometimes, it's useless.
But you say something anyway.

Smile.
Or don't smile.

Both ways are correct?
Sometimes.

I MISS YOU RIGHT THIS MINUTE. I JUST DO.

it's okay to go ahead and let myself miss you
north of tucson in my mind
mine too now
once i tried to run
to a point in the sky

too far up up up up
big stones and brush
with fierce stickers

heading for heaven
it was not scorched
breath running deep

limits everywhere
and need for strength
is endless endless

who knows though
rugged steep stone trail
straight up the catalinas

might be just the way
to bypass heaven
and reach the very top

endless miles of nowhere
and just the place
where place is place

BONE-DEEP GLADNESS

A Tiny Note From Red Petal Girl And My Own Notes

when you leave vietnam especially hanoi please bring me a memory
of trees growing and growing   all trees grown back especially those
bombed into oblivion by my nation

my nation   i have to say my nation   tried to obliterate hanoi because my nation
does not know what to do with its own painful shit history memory misery   how
could it know how to find out from questions not asked . . . not daring to know

a sacred land it is   but i do not know exactly why and how it is   i just
know   and let it be knowledge forever   a way to salvation not through
forgiveness   but the only way possible to accept honesty and true . . .

pain

an acceptance I have to fight myself to understand   why   why   why   is
asked over and over again by me and others who need foes to hate and fear   lose
that hate and fear   and you/will come to accept at last

this is the knowledge necessary   i/my nation cannot seem to let my fear and hate
to let go   and forget   but i/my nation have/has to at last

. . . please i/we must

red boy works for hours going crazy
you know type this type that going nuts
a word then delete a word what the fuck
is this the way the world works shit shit
shit and more shit red boy feels like blue
you know too much of this crazy work
Is not good for anybody so call it a night

okay good night
and i miss you red petal girl
i know i do i admit it
red boy says yeah poems they are and stories too that's what really makes the
world go round
and round

NOT TOO SOON A POEM COMES LIKE THE EVENING STAR

SO FAR FAR AWAY

poem words tumbling over each other stumbling
leaping flying hopping and stumbling again again
that's what poems do and singing and laughing yelling
rhyming once in a while squinting from time to time

white black orange blue green yellow silver gold copper
stone and metal colors and sky colors blue blue blue
blue and gray gray icy gray in november idaho
or deep misty distant gray dark tumble twisty dakota sky

november especially coming from nebraska border hills
it's gonna snow already snow in wyoming sky talks thinks
colder like sudden memory of last year happens too soon
poems of october become chilly by thanksgiving evening

coming from tom, jenny, and their kids home eight miles
or so south of rosebud the dakota hills at night icy looking
already with just a slight wind moving the pines and oaks
good day good way our journeys hold true toward winter

not too soon a poem comes like the evening star so far far
west yes beyond kansas our journeys toward winter are here:
prairie night is close and far we head toward and beyond
one journey is a poem another poem is from here to there

words upon words are the stones steps breaths pauses
we come upon poems waiting in the next valley and hill
when we get there we'll know words have been waiting still

like always ready for tumbling stumping into our stories

Looking toward the Sangre de Cristo Mountains across the valley, I can't see much of the mountains because there are clouds upon clouds. Thick white clouds upon mid-slopes and upper peaks and behind the mountains.

Peh-eh-chah, I say to myself. Peh-eh-chah. Let it rain; we need rain; we want rain; we love rain.

I hope it will rain. I pray it will. It's been in the high 90s temperature-wise the past 2 days here in Santa Fe.

Since you're in California now, please send some rain this way. And when the Kahtzinah come next week to Aacqu, I will thank them. And thank them for heeding your thought-word for rain here in Santa Fe and Aacqu.

You should see the rain there.
Sometimes you can see the Shiwana step off Shra'kaiyah in soft and gentle white rain clouds.

And come patiently, even slowly, slowly come toward the valley in which Aacqu sits.

The stone walls of the sandstone promontory mesa wait.

The hot yellow, brown, and red stone walls ready for the rain.

Breezes and gusts of wind always precede the rain,
even before the Shiwana descend into the valley.

Sometimes the people impatiently say, I wish the wind wouldn't blow
so much, all that dust and sand, like we don't get enough sand and wind!

Without the preceding wind blowing, the rain will not arrive.

Finally, though, into the Aacquumeh valley, the Shiwana come.

White misty rain and thunder now.

Booming thunder peals from Shra'kaiyah mountain.

And from Deenih-buuh, the forested high mesa bluffs to the west.

And even from Kaweshtima thirty or so miles to the north—

Thunderstorm it may not be yet but it's rain.

Peh-eh-chah!

Peh-eh-chah!

The People say and the songs-prayers say: as the Kahtzinah Shiwana dance and
sing in the plaza.

The dusty ground is hot and swirls of dust dance.

Beautiful rain is arriving. Beautiful rain is here.

Beautiful rain loves. Beautiful we love.

Thankful, we are. Thankful we are.
Dancing and singing and breathing, we welcome the rain.

Peh-eh-chah! Peh-eh-chah!

It is almost time for me to go to work this morning. As I head toward the Sangre
de Cristo mountain foothills, I will be singing Peh-eh-chah!

Beautiful rain will come! It is coming!

I send you rain and rain songs. And love.
Listen, you can hear the Shiwana singing rain songs
and you can see them dancing: the rain is coming!

The rain is here now!

WRITING AN ANTI-WAR POEM

July 19, 2014

again? seriously? again? yeah, again?

no more war?

no more war?

no more war?

what then? repeat?: what the hell then?

not nuke the middle east?

pull the plugs on russia and the usa?

confuse the chinese?: capitalism doesn't work?

send tea partyers of the world to hell?

what then? repeat: what the hell then?

aaaarrrrrgh? aaaaaarrrrrrgh? whimper and weep?

hell no hell no hell no hell no! Hellll NOOOO!

ALREADY JULY 30, 2014?

I can't believe it.

I don't want to believe it.

Yet I do believe it.

It is today.

And I better believe it.

Time passes. Fast. And what in the world does that mean?

One minute in June I'm in Tempe. Next minute I'm in Santa Fe.

Different days. Different places. Maybe even different planets?

Who knows? I do. Hmmmmm. I think.

This morn my hour run: 5:30 to 6:30. South Mountain foothills.

Halfway up, the sun came busting over Superstition Mountain horizon. Thank you, I say, motioning with my hand and mouth to Creation.

Morning sunlight bursts through trees nearby and over rooftops. Asphalt street under my feet. I can feel the hard surface.

Breathe. Breath is pretty good. Tired but not bad. No one around. No dogs barking. Birds chirping though.

Thank everything all around. Motion with hand again. South Mountain foothills and me.

I feel very fortunate. Thanking Creation. So I have to put that into the algebra of this morning.

I remember a melody I was playing on the piano yesterday afternoon. And I try to hum it as I run.

But it doesn't work, somehow it doesn't quite match the rhythm of my running. My running rhythm doesn't match the melody.

Turn into Saguaro Park East, a slight rise, and a couple of female and male couples up ahead. I pass them.

Half mile or so to the main entry and I'm thinking perhaps I'll go farther than I did yesterday.

But now i'm hot since the sun is out and away from the horizon and the trees and housetops,

and full sunlight pushes on my back, shoulders, and head,

and I'm breathing hard. So I tell myself to relax you're not racing anyone. Well, good, I say and try to relax.

But I slow up a bit and I'm self-conscious about it, so I get back into faster pace and start counting again.

Until I reach the area where people park their cars.

And the gate to the park is just beyond.

Someone is unpacking his bicycle from his car trunk and nods at me.

I wave and feel my breath full and strained and I want to relax again but don't.

I pass through the gate. Dirt, gravel, sand, and stones begin here.

Some time back, I used to go down a little trail to the arroyo below and run on the sand.

But it's slow and hard going in the loose sand and there are buried sticks and stones in the sand.

I don't even think of going down there now. You have to be in super shape to do that!

So I go a little ways up the regular trail and decide I'm going to turn around.

And do. And breathing is much easier now.

The fully risen sun helps me to know I am alive.

Dawah eh is my greeting. Thank you is my prayer.

Thank you, Dzah-yaayuutyah, our Creator-Provider.

What a way to start this day.

WHEN WE WERE KIDS

We used to go down to the chuu'nah and play.
That's what we called the river, no wider than 6 or 7 feet across.
Except when it flooded during rainy season in July and August.

No internet then.

Just kids that we were and the river.
And dragonflies. Blue, yellow, red, green ones. All gorgeous.
And mud that was black, brown, gooey, smelly, fun to play in!
Getting slick mud all over us. Faces and hair, hands, feet, clothes.

And birds, butterflies, ants, water spiders, snakes.
And minnows flashing in shallow rapids.
And frogs and trout, of course.

No way was there even anything like internet.

Imagination was our power and our spirit.
Nothing else but. Our reality.

Being alive, being kids!
O ooooo so alive alive alive, and more alive.
More than anything ever alive, ever ever and ever.

Quails came by and made me smile. They make me laugh the way they're always talking and planning what to do.

Quails talking and planning what to do.

Like Red Boy.

Conspirators.

Told you.

Talking. Planning. Plotting. Conspirators.

Figuring. Might as well.

Like nobody's business but theirs.

I wonder what they've got in mind.

Quails used to come around our corn crib.

Dozens of them in flocks.

They'd pick up the corn kernels in the sand that'd fallen off the cobs.

White, red, blue, yellow kernels.

Fluffing their feathers,

Kicking dirt aside,

Chirpy chuckling like they do. Chirping.

Maybe sing a song or two.

And when we'd walk up they would flutter away like they do.

Low-flying flutter some yards away into the wah-ahspah bushes.

All around them and us, the blue sky.

And the mountains' magical look touching them and us.

VIEWS FROM SHTAA'MAH—MY HOME—WHERE I GREW UP

Rinconado Canyon to the north.

Diablo Canyon to the south and slightly southwest.

At the place where the canyon curves eastward, my Dad's Uncle Comman'do-shaatah had his sheep camp.

South of there, at the foot of tall sandstone cliffs, there was a sweet-tasting spring with water that also had a touch of juniper roots.

Across the canyon's sandy plain with cactus mostly was where Miinah Kquuyow—Old Woman Salt—lived.

Mom would say, "Every time you pass by where she lives, you have to give her cornmeal. Don't forget."

And she would add, "If you don't, Nahtrahnee will blow and blow."

She meant Nahtrahnee's winds will blow you and your house down if you don't offer Miinah Kquuyow prayers with cornmeal.

So you had to dig into your cornmeal pouch and take out a pinch
and give it to Miinah Kquuyow, no matter what!

Probably even quails have to give cornmeal to her, no matter what!

Isn't that something?

TINY TINY HEART LIKE A SEED

you plant the seed
rain waters it
once twice thrice and so on
a tiny plant comes greenly
oh yes oh my so green
so new a life
tiny wind singing
a bird hears and joins in
oooiiuuu ooowhoaaa hmmm
vibration like creation
mini-seconds, seconds, minutes on on on

a tiny seed heart like nobody's business

blooms into yellow purple red
flowers hearts like flowers

WHEN YOU'RE HERE IN SEPTEMBER LET'S FIND

A DESERT SPOT

when it's going to rain and we'll wait for rains to come
and we will take off our clothes when rain comes hard
laughing holding our faces and hands and hearts open
letting the rain receive us as we holler peh eh chah peh eh chah peh eh chah let it
rain let it rain let it rain!

JUST AN OLD STORY YOU MIGHT KNOW ALREADY

But we can call it a cricket and crow and coyote story: cricket and crow were sitting on a rock near the edge of a canyon   they were singing   *crah crah* crow sang   *kirkirpree kirkirpree* cricket sang they saw coyote coming up the canyon trail below them   *crah crah* there's coyote said crow   *kirkirpree kirkirpree* where where said cricket   *crah crah* there there said crow

all of a sudden there was coyote right below them in the canyon   he was looking all around himself but he could see no one singing *crah crah* like crow does or *kirkirpree kirkirpree* like cricket does   coyote did not look up   he just kept turning his head east and west and north and south

crah crah I'll send him a message said crow   *kirkirpree kirkirpree* okay do so said cricket   then crow shit little dark beads that fell fell fell fell down Into the canyon below where coyote was looking east west north and south *bam bam bam bam* the little dark shit beads went when they hit coyote in the noggin   *crah crah* said crow here we are   *kirkirpree kirkirpree* said cricket here we are

crah crah here we are again said crow   *kirkirpree kirkirkpree* said cricket here we are again   *crah crah* ha ha ha said crow   *kirkirpree kirkirpree* said cricket ha ha ha

yep sounds just like red boy coulda been there too riiiiiight! you bet.

FREEDOM AND THE LIE

Monticello And Thomas Jefferson And The Plan

Freedom. Land. Water. Plants. Air. Mother Earth.
Freedom. Body. Food. Growth. Earth Mother. Life.

Word as rhetoric is easy. Enough is easy. Too easy.
Really. Intellect and the land—that's where the test is.
Thomas Jefferson never begged for water. Never argued
for it. Never thanked Indigenous Peoples. I'm sure.

Freedom is a mindset. It is plan: sought and decided.
Not negotiated. Jefferson was law. Plan. According to him
and God, air was his. Plan. Therefore Monticello had no need
or justification at all. Plan. With no permission. Nor obligation.

Freedom is never its own. Monticello was constructed.
Simple fact & act. Indigenous Peoples and Mother Earth died.
Freedom's constructions stand and will stand as law stands.
Until the lie-law undermines, undermines, undermines its own.

I DON'T QUITE KNOW

saturday night already
what happened to this morning and this day
i don't quite know
i've been tired for some reason all day
and an upset stomach
i don't know the reason for my loose stomach
haven't run for days now
not since early last week
and the days have sped by

i wish for dragonflies
to see them
send a couple this way okay
perhaps phoenix valley is too hot for dragonflies or too far away
yeah that's probably why

pigeons out on the grass in front though pecking
pecking at stuff in the grass
i try to see what they're finding
pecking pecking
but i don't see anything among the blades of grass

i have to finish up my syllabus by tomorrow
since I finished only part of one
and the other still has to be done
a prof's work is never done
what am i doing here anyway
i ask for the millionth time

the truth is actually more than the tenth millionth time
sometimes i feel like just stopping teaching
just stop teaching
simple as that

at the end of this week i.e. friday
i was exhausted just plain tired
i am not that old i thought but i was tired
and just wanted to sleep sleep

and i did a bit more than i usually do
and it felt okay
like i cheated no one

i miss you
i do

NIGHT SKY DREAMING ALL THE WAY BEYOND THE MILKY WAY

milky way dreaming remembers red boy alive and well
july, august, september, october all summer into fall
at the hesperus foot of the southern rocky mountain edge
a little valley with rio de la plata west of durango, colorado

august was rainy so often that year rainy days with sun
and all that night sky space when it was so clear no clouds
forever one can see more than once in a lifetime and more
black night sky sparkling trembling moaning pleasantly i think

(By the way, today I received the Chinese sugar you sent. For the ginger tea I'll make.
I'll have to get a root though. Just slice or dice and boil. Right? And add the sugar.)

it was the very first time I ever saw so much night sky
in colorado or anywhere so much because of the mountains
that opened my mind-soul ability and function to see to see
distance distance and space and feel breath beyond oxygen

and more than air and wind and beginning and ending
but breath as beyond measure like stars are also points
like guides on journeys here to there to wherever you head
star light star way star right and left point that way and go

from within the tipi through the smoke hole i'd peer steady
and gaze straight up and see light years that meant nothing
unless you believed in the speed of light—what?—accepting
truth that's dependent on measurement and units of time—

say what?—i'd hitchhiked to north carolina earlier that summer
and i'd believe everything was like forever: it wasn't measured
from hesperus to pembroke or to mars or acoma or heaven
it was being able to see with ability and the function to see

oh my yes i was happy to know there was so much night sky

GIVING RECEIVING GIVING

Dragonfly
Eagle

Of life
These gifts of being

Their colors and the way they fly
Their movements when they fly

That's what matters
That is the breathing in
That is the breathing out

When you offer cornmeal in prayer and honor
In reverence
You breathe in
You breathe out

And you place the cornmeal on the ground
Breathing in
Breathing out

That's what matters

WITH LOVE AND AWE

words are floating in the ocean and sky
In the blood and sweat of the breath and wind
in ache and relief in eye and toe
in everything and everywhere

isn't it wonderful words are making us float
and bleed and sweat with breath and wind
aching and blinking with happiness even our eyes and toes
and come come come to us gently and kindly so

at mid-day coming from tucson up the hill above casa grande
i can see all the way into the sky over china and i can see you
wandering around in awe and love of life there where you are
and the life over this way too with a big smile and plain old glee

thank you i say red petal girl i miss you and you take care okay

MOON CROON BY RED BOY

A POEM FOR JACK HIRSCHMAN

Moon moon this morning
Moon as I was climbing the fence
Moon sitting on top of the house across the street
Moon that is naayaa to many

Moon morning that is 5:20 clock time
Moon doesn't count time
Moon to light the world
Moonlight shhhhhh light light light

Moon mentions antonin artaud
Moon-odd sense of life
Moon minds its own
Moonlight lights on artaud's face

Moon-mention this morning
Moon and theatre with cast of 420 plus
Moon, my interest in theatre goes back to college
Moon and artaud's imagination as reality

Moon dreams   Thoughts   Delusions   Realities
Moon no less real than reality
Moon light and dark jack hirschman did a book
Moon called artaud anthology publisher city lights

Moon was maybe naayaa to artaud
Moon who knows dark who knows light as real real real
Moon tonight i'll look for
Moon morning will come real as reality always

FOREVER IS TRUE?

Yes, I remember: "Forever is true." Even repetitions are true.
Sands, sands, sands, so many grains, too many to keep track;
they made the world countless; so true, same with forgetters.

Facts are ever-evolving and ever-multiplying baby snakes.
Under the deep waters so deep, deep, deeper, even deeper.
And above that as in above our need for numbers is space.

In space? Is space? Space we can't measure, just live within.
Space so much, so endless, horizons are means of vision,
so space, endless, makes endless sense like air breathing air.

Living as breath each intake and outtake again, again, again.
Ahh yes, above that is beyond, here hold your hand up, up, up,
and fingers pointed up with your little finger on the Big Dipper

and thumb on the Evening Star and Sun too close for comfort.
Orange-red-yellow, fierce flares forever, even memory burns
instantly-constantly away, tattoos take, making lasting futures.

Memory's too soon though. Red Boy heard that. But you know,
he's so gullible his own Mom says. She says with a hmmmph,
"And says he heard, 'Forever is true.' He should talk, hmph."

TURNS

red petal girl
turns into a zither

because its sound
became her bones and face

people turn their heads
when she passes by

i can't forget that wind
ever ever forever returning

red petal girl love is power
and how songs are made

never forget bones and face
moon knows that song

zither knows that song too
when she passes by

MEMORY

Not far from our home in Deetseyamah—McCartys in English—there's a mulberry tree my Grandpa Maayai-shaatah planted near the river—chuu'nah in Aacqumeh niiyah—many, many years ago, probably when he and my Grandma moved their family from Aacqu down to the Rio de San Jose river valley. It was a beautiful tree about eight feet tall when I was growing up. It had light green leaves that would start to appear in early spring, probably in March. And we would wait expectantly for the pink berries. Green berries at first that we'd go and check frequently, every day in fact, to see if they were soon turning pink. The berries would take days and days and more days to turn from green to pink. They were pale green for the longest time. Weeks I figured, much later on. So we'd wait and wait some more. We, as in us kids and the birds. Because birds would fly to the mulberry tree and check it out too. Finally though after such a long, long time of waiting, the berries would turn a little pink and we would discuss whether the berries were ready to eat. Or not. We were told by our parents, "No, wait a few days more." Meaning forever. That's what it felt like, those little pale green berries slowly, so slowly turning pink. Finally when they were more pink than green we thought we could pick one berry, just one if we could keep ourselves from getting more, and taste it. So a cousin, Lucy, who was older than me and her little sister by a year, was the one to pick and taste. We all watched her, mesmerized or hypnotized by her face and mouth, taking all the time in the world moving her mouth and lips and her tongue inside. "Tell us then," my little brother practically hollered, "Is it ready to eat?" Almost sadly, Lucy said, "Nope, not quite ready. It's still sour. Needs to get sweeter." Forever, that's what it felt like to me. Waiting forever. Still a little sour but growing slowly sweeter. Finally the day would come when we would pick a wholly pink mulberry and eat it and it would be sweet. Perfect! All that waiting, all that time, all the tortuous time waiting for the mulberry tree to be ready for picking and eating. "Hurry, before the birds get all of them!" I can imagine the birds telling each other, "Hurry before the kids pick them all!" And it took about two days for the berries to be picked from the beautiful, pale green-leafed mulberry tree down by the bend in the chuu'nah.

That's one of my favorite all-time memories of growing up in Deetseyamah.

FLYING RED PETAL GIRL

fly fly

fly   fly   fly

horizon

ocean

mountain

desert

                    fly   fly   flyyyyyyyyyyyyyyy

a butterfly

red yellow brilliant blue

a humming bird

green shimmering velvet

whirr

                whirrrrr

                                    whirrrrrrrrr. . .

rrring

TECHNOLOGY TRAPPINGS & GRANDMOTHER SPIDER

koocheenih-naakuh had run away from her husband who imprisoned her in his
rock cliff house high above the desert that stretched for miles all around

her husband was away to play with his friends thunder and lightning beings when
she had somehow managed to escape down rock cliffs

and now koocheenih-naakuh was running as fast and hard as she could toward her
home village far away across the vast desert and she was very tired and afraid

because she could hear her husband and his friends carousing with their thunder
roaring and fierce lightning flashing in the western sky

aai aiiyaaah ah she cried i'm never going to get back home to my village from
where my husband stole me *aaaaiii aiyah aaah* she wept and wept

because her legs and feet were no longer able to walk she stopped *aaaaiiiiaiyaaaah*
skuchaiyuumah she wept and wept looking at the western sky full of giant and
dark thunderclouds

koocheenih-naakuh sat on a stone not knowing what to do but
to weep and look at thunderclouds coming closer and closer

she was frantic with worry and sorrow and pity and fear
for herself and she could hear her husband roar like thunder THERE SHE IS I
SEE HER!

koocheenih-naakuh put her head on her knees closed her eyes tightly and put her
hands over her ears so she wouldn't hear her furious husband

then suddenly koocheenih-naakuh heard a little voice saying dya-ow why are you
weeping with sadness and sitting here do you need help

koocheenih-naakuh opened her eyes and took her hands from her ears but she could only see huge thunderclouds and her husband atop them

and she heard his huge thunderous roar THERE SHE IS I WILL KILL HER and koocheenih-naakuh was totally panicked with fear and she didn't know what to do

look down this way granddaughter dyah-ow duwehnuu chu-ookah
the little voice said and this time koocheenih-naakuh clearly heard
she looked down and saw a little bitty spider at her feet look down
this way the little voice said and sing with me duwehnuu chu-ookah
duwehnuu come this way and sing with me

come into this hole where you will be safe from that skhuuyuu shruu'wee who keeps you imprisoned and makes you his slave

koocheenih-naakuh saw a tiny hole in the ground and saw she could not go in the little hole because she was too big no way she would fit

sing with me *duweh nuu duweh nuu newpuustiih kehnuu newpuustiih*
sing grandmother spider said *duweh nuuu duweh nuuu newpuustiih*

with the power of the song that koocheenih-naakuh sang with dyah-ow kahmaah'skquh—this way in this way in i will enter in this way this is the way i will enter in—koocheenih-naakuh became smaller, littler, tiny, and tinier and she was able to enter into the little hole

now koocheenih-naakuh was safe thanks to dyah-ow kahmaah'skquh who you can call upon to help you out . . . especially with traditional cultural technology hey hey yah haaa-ah

Hihdruutsi doesn't remember all of it just now but that's the way it goes!

ALWAYS MEMORY. JAKE, ME, YOU, YOUTH, A CHORE AND TASK.

At 9 years of age, I was totally impressed. Totally.
Jake's art power. The moment was total. Reddish brown
sorrel horse. I was totally swept into the power of Jake.
Sheen and silky. Dark and shiny eyes. Omigosh.

Swept into the power that Jake was. Cahwaa'yuh.
To a boy. A horse is a horse. And a boy is a boy.
A beautiful cahwaa'yuh, Jake was. Beauty is a power.
No reason here. Reasoning is true, at once its own.

Daddy must have ridden Jake down to Dahskah.
Where our cornfields were. Mama drove the wagon.
We went to hoe weeds and weeds in the corn rows.
Hard hot summer work hoeing weeds. Jake nearby.

Daddy also piled soil around corn stems and roots.
Sculpting—in my memory—like building a house wall.
An artist gently forming life from Dahskah's dark soil.
Mama and I hoeing weeds. Me stealing looks at Jake.

Sky alit so blue, blue. Alit on Jake's beauty as a horse.
Corn green and growing taller, breeze rustling leaves.
Holy directions: north, east, south, west, above, below.
Mother, Father, Child: held safely, carefully, lovingly.

Kaweshtima, sacred mountain to the north, Symbol
of the Beginning, fields of corn, squash, melons, hay
where Dahskah is a floodplain. Dawaa-eh to ancestors
still protective, teaching, caring, providing for all of us.

My Grandpa Mah'yai-shaatah planted here before us,
and I'm sure Grandma was here with him some days.
Mah'yai, a healer, a medicine man, was skilled, trusted.
Grandma, creative potter, mother of eight daughters.

Dahskah will be the way it was when I was just a boy.
Memory is a chore and task true. Always and forever.
As always, Jake too will be there. Beautiful as always.
He will still be Daddy's horse, one "too wild to ride."

That's what Mama'd say, and Daddy would just laugh.
As I tell my children, grandchildren, great-grandchildren,
they'll laugh too. And you, my love, will be beautiful too
like love always—a chore and task true—always love.

CRYSTAL. CHRYSTALS.

I think another thing about life that's a huge gift is that it's possible to go back. To take oneself back to a place of pain at a later date, when you are both the same person and a different person.

Some things you say or write are crystals. Stark. Very present. Bright. Open. In plain sight. Sometimes beautiful, sometimes not. Clarity within.

I've never wanted to go back into pain.
Because of fear.
Because I am afraid of pain.
I've felt physical pain.
Feeling of pain is vibrant and fierce.
In fact, a ferocious veering unrestrained.
I can't describe the sensation of bearing unbearable pain.
Not turning away at all.
Insane drive, even a desire?
Perhaps so, a magnetic sort.
Being drawn to unbearable pain is inexplicable.

Emotional pain is different because it is confusing.
And nuanced.
Ambiguous even, too intellectual.
Children unclear about pain.
I never knew what to do with it.
Fear is even more apparent and obvious.
Fear is even more apparent and obvious.

LANGUAGE DANCING. MAYBE.

Letting language dance.
Letting language become a dance.
Letting language dance and teach you to dance.
Letting dancing and teaching become the knowledge they are.

Sometimes when I speak the Aacqumeh dzeh'nee I let it go
so that its meaning is the power it moves with. That is, the meaning
is apparent in my mind-speech-purpose so that it moves with power.
The power of the meaning. The power of comprehension.
Even when I sometimes feel uncertain about its meaning.

It works though when meaning is communicated by its motion.

Power is in the motion/action.

Dance is like that; songs are signals. Sometimes rhetorical meaning is indicated;
meaning is there.
Sometimes. And other times, meaning is in the dance movements
and the body follows.
Arms, hands, shoulders. Eyes, toes, feet, knees, thighs, legs, hips. Power of motion.
Energy = meaning.

Song and dance are a collaboration. Rattles, turtle shells around ankles, bells
tinkling. All sounds are dancing.
I used to Deer Dance when I was a teenager. Light prancing steps, dip shoulders,
swivel hips, turn with toes.
Following drum beats, following beats closely, following voice rhythms and pitches
up and down.

Word sounds. Movement. Actualizing self in song and meaning as you are always
essential to the song.

Letting language dance.

Letting language become a dance.

Letting language dance and teach you to dance.

Letting dance and teaching become the knowledge they are.

Maybe that's how translation works. When I think about it that is the way it works.

THAT GIRL

I think of you as that girl below. *As a girl.* Words are made from whatever/context you are in. *Crumbled in my palms* squatting or sitting or crouching *by a pond.*

After the world was put together by Iatiku, Nautsiti *walked across the grass and the feather ball waited there, soft-soft.*

I don't know what bird the feathers come from. My son's Acoma name is Dyaamih Hihshuunih which means: soft underbelly feathers of Eagle.

Maybe the soft feathers came from some bird around there. *Soft-soft.*
Maybe even a Dyaamih.

As a girl, sometimes I sat on the dried mud by a pond, picking up pieces of dried mud. Flat shapes made when earth cracks itself. Sometimes the pieces crumbled in my palms, sometimes I lifted a small corner and a whole piece came, solid, together, still wet on the underside. Dirt belly. It made me smile. Sometimes I rubbed the mud on my own skin.

At the ceremony when the Kahtzinah come for four days beginning on Friday, I will think of you by a pond. Drought or no drought.

Just after I swam. And thought of Ceremony having saved my life so many times. I came up for air and hummingbird flew right over my head. After weeks of not coming. Then I got out of the pool, walked across the grass, and the feather ball waited there. Soft-soft.

I will think of Nautsiti. Rubbing the mud on her skin.

Red Petal Girl *lifted a small corner and a whole piece came, solid, together, still wet on the underside, dirt belly.*

FIG

a beautiful fig
looks delicious

beyond the definition of delicious
grace light and joyfulness

breathe love in and feel
it dissolve throughout

toes heels knees hips ribs
stomach heart shoulder lungs

eye brain forehead awe
become grace light and fig

good night now and sleep well
smile again with grace joy fig

HIHDRUUTSI & TUZIGOOT ROCK LIZARDS REMEMBER

they move like rock lizards then
zip this way then zip that way
one second in your bright eye
next second way outta sight

then suddenly again peeking
from under dry tumbleweed
shadow partly by its striped skin
then in its invisible next flash

an eye in your late eye faster
than any thought right there
steady on the rock of your nose
staring straight stark light quick

into your eye deeply striking
remembrance for a million years
of yesterday in a second leap that
can only be forever and ever ever

WHAT IS THE SHAPE OF A LEAF?

Quite simple, Thomas will likely say.

it is the shape of green
it is the shape of a question
it is the shape of a poem
it is the shape of chengdu
and intensity
and mystery
and magic
and wonder

no wonder then there is green intensity
no wonder then there is a question of mystery
no wonder then there is a poem of magic
no wonder then there is a chengdu of wonder

quite simple then the shape of a leaf is green
quite simple then the shape of a question is mystery
quite simple then the shape of a poem is magic
quite simple then the shape of chengdu is wonder

but what shall we do with intensity when it stands by the river
and the river keeps moving and moving
why i think we shall let it be mystery magic wonder all in one and it will be okay
for the river to keep moving moving moving

This poem above is by Red Boy who is also hihdruutsi and also don't forget he's
The Boy Who Went to Live in a Goat Cave Once And Forever.

REX BARKING AT THE MAGPIES

the '72 summer Rex and I were the lone
occupiers at Hesperus Liberation Camp
when Fort Lewis College Indigenous
students started their own college

Rex barking at the magpies:

rar rar rar rarity rar rarrrrra rooa rarp rarp

Rex barking at the moon:

ra ra ra ra rawr rawr roooorp rooorp rooooaaaah

Rex barking at me:

rararararooo rararararoo row row row ahaaa

Magpies. Moon. Me. Quizzical quiet faces; we have nothing to say. Well, except for
one magpie who says: *kerrak kerrak howk ark yuuukr*

Isn't that so damn cool?

A LONG TIME AGO STORY

At sheep camp many years ago,
Uncle Roy—the one who used to live in China Town—said,
I had a horse by the name of Lightning.
Well, one time at dusk we went to see Stella who lived near Staawaawaakuh where
the chuu'nah turns to the south
and there are very tall cottonwood trees growing there.

By the time Lightning and I got to where Stella lived
it was dark night. Nothing but stars all over the sky.
Stella lived with her parents and I had to get her attention.
So I pretended to be a Tsuush'kih and went *Aaaruuuu-arf-arf-aarrfu* but nothing
happened. Then I went *Aaaarfff aaarfff eeaaahooo.*

Lightning looked at my wide open mouth and at my shoes,
then shook his head and sputtered with his horse lips and looked away with a horse
laugh of all things!

Finally though a back door of the house opened. I could see a dim light inside. It
was Stella and she came toward the alfalfa field that was near her house.

And I said to Lightning, Wish me luck, and went to meet Stella.

Lightning didn't even look at me because he was happily eating alfalfa in the field.

And I didn't even get to hear the rest of the story I wanted so much to hear.

Oh well, another day, another dollar. Or something like that.

QUESTION YES & NO

Where's the best blues in Beijing?
I should have asked Amiri Baraka that question.
And he would've laughed that edgy wild laugh he had.
Hahaaaaah ha, the blues in Beijing! And punched his knee.

I don't know if Amiri ever made it to Beijing though.
When he was young and LeRoi Jones then . . . and I was barely a teen,
I loved his enthusiasm and daring.
Plays, writing plays, wanting to be a playwright, that was his passion.

Blues for Mr. Charlie, that was Baldwin.
But Amiri was the blues for Mr. Charley alright.

I'd heard of him and his writing in early progressive Southern writing then. From
Black Mountain College poets Robert Creeley, Charles Olson, Ed Dorn. When he
changed his name to Amiri from LeRoi who knew who he'd become.

Not Mr. Charley.

Since Amiri was from the blues he was always the blues. "From" was in for Baraka.

Blues is everywhere. Beneath, beyond, before. And after after.

The Blues.

The best blues in Beijing is where Red Boy would be. Yeah right there in the beat.
The beat. The Amiri Baraka beat.

CRICKETS

i haven't seen or heard a cricket all summer long since july already
except for the one just now brother earl carried outdoors at acoma
it may be too hot for crickets in phoenix maybe too hot for outdoors

i miss them though cricketing away here and there and everywhere
it's like they are invisible and their chirping keeps them invisible
ha   i bet you never heard that theory of cricket invisibility   yeah   yeah

blackfeet storyteller told me that once it's a true saying that's why
chirping chirping chirping makes them invisible no lie   old story
you hear one right by your shoe and you look and nothing's there

chirp chirp it's over there by that rock and you go look but nothing
chirping and chirping driving you crazy pretty soon it's over there
you look but nothing you can't see them right in front of your eyes

chirp chirp over here over there no not there   right here by the bush
chirp-per-ti-chirrrrp chirp like right by your shoe   see they're invisible
like—old woman old man—they said   crickets are invisible by chirping

WHAT IF

what if words
are light

they are
and we are

jake wild and fast
goats and their cave
a boy afraid but aware

a girl who breathes-dances
and notices everything:
mother father sister friend
who wants to die who dies

what if light
was not a word
how to dance then
how to see then
how to know fear then

hihdruutsi as red boy sometimes
says what if

SEVEN TSINAH

1.

o my how grow tsinah
how grow oceans
how grow planets

2.

do we know
should we know
must we know

3.

are these the little ones
ones we saw months ago
ones with their mother

4.

what do we learn
what are we taught
do we learn what and why

5.

when it rains are we thankful
when tsinah dance do we
when tsinah talk do we know

6.

days and times are ours to know
ours to know the tsinah
dancing talking are theirs and ours

7.

peh eh chah ah aneh eh dawaa-eh
peh eh chah ah aneh eh dawaa-eh
neh chaaah ah guuu uuh uuuuuuuh

TSUNUUNUU'GAH

i think you're talking about
a gentle, gentle constant rain

when you look east toward kakai'yah
the tsunuunuu'gah turns the mesa into a cloud

tsunuunuu'gah raindrops are misty
and very fine teeny droplets on the skin

to the northwest horse mesa is invisible
except for its highest lava cliffs barely seen

i can smell osmanthus in tsunuunuu'gah
you can't see it but you know it's there

BEAUTY AS TURQUOISE

stone
stoned
stony

beauty in the mind in the eye
beauty in the moment in space
beauty always and ever

stone mountain
stone river
stone lake

beauty as ever
beauty as dawn
beauty as starlight

stony
stoned
stone

       turquoise is my name she said and what's yours
       sam he said who named you he asked
       grandpa mike she said grandpa mike said turquoise was pretty
       yes sam said blue blue blue is beautiful he nodded

       sam looked at her and he didn't say anything
       sam she said who gave you your name
       i don't know he said no one told me maybe no one knows
       do you want to know she said and looked at sam

       yes i do he said i don't know who to ask
       your mom turquoise said or your dad she said
       they're gone i think died he said i've heard
       oh she said and was quiet and she said oh again

a turquoise moment

AWAKE ALL NIGHT

not me i sleep
dreams are mystery and wonder

fate a feature of reality
star quilts are gifts of art

i am not on the moon
this is silver city a town in new mexico with high curbs

some time ago marlene's uncle bunk's buddy found a seed pot
somewhere here with pumpkin and corn seeds sealed inside of it

another time he found another pot
it had purple seeds beans he said

later the buddy planted the beans and they grew six feet tall
lo and behold he said the beans in its pods were purple as the pope's pajamas

awake all night is not always good
sometimes though sometimes it's okay

no matter i sleep i sleep finally until 4:30 am
i look out the window between the blinds and the morning is still night

PRAYER

dragonfly is prayer
before and after it lands
on your arm or soul for a moment with you

a prayer like dragonfly is its own life
seeking what it knows—and
accepting is finding

DREAMS AND REALITY

in the dream of the red chamber, the boy, jia baoyu, is born with a stone in his
mouth
magic jade

I heard my eldest sister tell a story about the boy who couldn't talk and he was
almost four years of age   so she and her two younger sisters went to their
grandfather who was a chaiyaanih, a healer, and told him their little brother was
not able to talk   and would he please come and help him so he could talk   their
grandpa said maybe he has nothing to say   grandpa grandpa please   come help
our beloved little brother to talk   we're afraid he's never going to talk   please
grandpa grandpa the girls cried   and so their grandpa went to the boy and said
to the boy naanah come here to me   and the boy did and stood in front of his
grandpa   open your mouth naanah   and the boy opened his mouth   and then
grandpa reached into his work jeans pocket and took a big brass key out of his
pocket and held it up for the boy and his sisters to see it   and then their grandpa
inserted the brass key into the boy's open mouth   and he turned the key with his
fingers like he was unlocking a door   and he said now naanah you will talk when
you're ready   and my sister turned to me and said ever since then we haven't
been able to keep his mouth shut!

maybe it was just a story   maybe it was a magic stone   i mean maybe it was a
magic key

ARTHUR THE CAT STARING WITH AN INTENSE MEDITATIVE GAZE

I wonder what Arthur sees?
I wonder what that "intense meditative gaze" means and consists of?
Good, bad, or indifferent?

When elephants look at human beings, do they have good thoughts?
I mean, do they see kind, considerate, generous, smart, and good beings?
Do they think well of people and do people look like people think they look like?

We had our horses Charley and Bill and they'd look at us kindly I think. And also with a sort of a curious look like horses have, a gaze I think that is something like human curiosity. They might lift their heads a bit and look away but then they return their gaze to you.

And they look and look. And you can almost see and feel their thoughts. I wonder what these beings are up to? Are they going to harness us and have us pull their wagon? Or will they give us dry hay? Or corn on the cobs we don't get often. Yes, I know, just more dry hay.

Do ants see us as giant beings that don't act too friendly lurching around not very gracefully?
I wonder what they see with their shiny and beady ant eyes?

Once in grade school, I put some red ants into a mason jar. Hundreds or thousands of other ants swarming all around my feet. Thousands of ants! I was going to take them to school with me the next day.

Those red ants probably thought I was a totally demented evil being trying to get them into the glass jar. They kept running and running. This way and that way, running, trying to get away from me.

Mostly they didn't want to come with me. To school? What in the world is that anyway? What's the world coming to?

So I wonder about Arthur the Cat looking, looking, looking at me and you meditatively.

I can never tell what's showing for sure on their faces. Except for ex-wife Agnes' pet Bushwhackit's face that grimaced into this fierce and deadly force of a kitty that attacked people.

I mean Bushwhackit stationed herself by the front door on the arm of this cheap sofa chair we had and when people walked through the doorway Bushwhackit leaped with a cat snarl, *raaaoooolwfff!*, not loudly but full of deadly curses that were totally bad news.

So whenever someone knocked or rang our door bell we had to rush to the door and holler, Wait, Wait I have to move Bushwhackit! And we had to move Bushwhackit from her attack chair, and Bushwhackit would fret and noisily hiss and spit at us as we put her on the floor.

Later though, we were sad when we had her burial behind the house in a weed patch of dirt bordered by a gravel and dirt alley way.

And, yeah, we fondly remembered Bushwhackit when Joe Eagle dressed in his powwow gear was attacked by her.

Funny? Yes, feathers flew here and there helter skelter! We laughed and chuckled and teased Joe about it later on!

HAVE YOU EVER HEARD OF A HORSE WHISPERER?

Maybe you're a horse whisperer.

My dad told me once or twice of people in Asia who talk with horses. Or speak a language that horses also speak.

Maybe it's like whispering or something that horses understand.
And there was that spring when Charley and Bill, our wagon and plow horses, fell into the cattle guard and were trapped. They couldn't get out. Their front legs were stuck between the heavy iron rails of the cattle guard.

A man heard their frantic horse screeches and painful shrieks and hoarse crying. On seeing them, the man didn't know what to do but he recognized Charley and Bill as our horses. So, in a hurry, he ran and walked to our home to tell Dad what had happened to our horses. Immediately, my dad went to where Charley and Bill were badly trapped in the cattle guard rails.

Charley and Bill were totally trapped, Dad said later. There was no way for them to get out. Totally trapped, my dad said several times. It looked impossible for them to get out. "When I heard them crying," he said, "I cried too. I couldn't help it. I love them; they are our relatives, our friends, and our helpers. Aahmoo-uh, ahmoo-uh, stah-waash'stiitrah." Beloved, beloved, our children.

"I had to help them, no matter what. I had to try. They were beloved. That is what matters. Try. No matter what.

"Impossible it may seem to be, but I had to try. Aahmoo-uh, they needed help. When I got there, Charley and Bill were crying with pain. They recognized me when I got there. I could tell from their eyes they were glad and happy to see me. When I saw their skin and flesh were scraped and torn down to the bones of their front legs, I could feel their pain. *Aaaiiieeee.*

"Somehow," Dad said, "who knows how but we have to do it. There was nothing else to do but to try. I told Charley and Bill that. Somehow we'll get you out. I told them. Both of you, I said."

Somehow, he got them out.

They were crying for help and from pain and hurt; Charley and Bill couldn't move much because their thick skin and muscle were torn and they were bleeding although some of it had stopped. "So I talked with them, I told them to be still as still as they could be and they grew quiet and only whimpered a little 'cause they were afraid and very afraid

"—and I was afraid—

"but they listened when I told them what I was going to do to help them, I would lift Bill's right foot first he had to just be still and relax so it wouldn't hurt so much and he relaxed enough although he was tense and he's very, very strong, and I told him I was being gentle and to please help me when I helped him slowly carefully gently lifted his right hoof up through the rail opening—I talked with them in Aacqumeh dzeh'niih eh Meh-de-gaanoh niiah so they could know what I was doing—and then it was Bill's other hoof the left one next in turn. I kept talking talking to Bill it's going to be alright it's going to be okay. Bill was trembling and shaking and afraid but he trusted my voice telling him it is going to be okay and Bill listened and kept listening until the other leg—the left one—and hoof was free.

"And then it was Charley's turn next to get his front legs free, *aii aiyah aah*, I said to myself out loud—and to the horses—Charley is bigger and heavier he had to listen to me—and turning my head I looked Charley in the face and asked him to help me. And I turned my look upward and said, Dzah-yaayuutyah, help us please, I ask this for all of us. I said, we can all do it together. Charley, you and Bill help me all the time when I ask you to help. So together with Dzah-yaayuutyah, we can do it by helping each other.

"Slowly, slowly, and carefully, Charley, lifting your foot and hoof up slowly and slowly we are doing it doing it we are doing it please help me and Bill we're praying and praying. Doing it by helping each other we can do it.

"Slowly and carefully very carefully patiently and carefully we can do it. Slowly, slowly by Charley's listening to my gentle and firm urging Charley helps me to talk softly and gently with my hand around his right hoof. Your foot and leg are heavy and you are strong and hurt but you are beloved, Charley, amooo-uh beloved, my child. Charley, beloved, help us to help you.

"And Charley brought his right foot up and I helped Charley put his hoof on a flat board I had brought to cover the open space between the iron rails. So he wouldn't fall back in. Talking softly and gently to his face and ears and eyes. And speaking softly with more feeling and with deeper feeling to Charley's soul, I felt his foot being freed.

"And then Charley had to move kaa'dyaamah—backward—away from the cattle guard. I said to Charley, 'Move backward, gaimeh'eh. kaa'dyaamah ah, please.' I spoke to Charley in da-ah dzehnee niah and also in Meh-de-gaanoh dzehnee niah to make sure he understood.

"Charley moved back a little ways and then some more backward away from the cattle guard. and so they, Charley and Bill, were freed now."

I shall always remember that experience my father had with Charley and Bill.

Maybe he was a horse whisperer. What do you think?

SALVATION OR ELSE

in 1996, when shery died, there was a severe drought in tucson. we'd all been waiting and waiting for the rain. you could see things starting to die. less baby animals that spring. i remember after she died, i prayed for rain, prayed and prayed and prayed for it. i felt like i was going to die if it didn't come. and after a few days, it did come. i ran outside barefoot. walked over the gravel in my parents' driveway, letting the rain soak me. the raindrops merging with my tears. two doves flew past me then. i always remember those doves.
that rain.
i knew i would be able to make it then.

1996. That was the first year of my sobriety. My sobriety that has been until now.
I sometimes don't know how I made it.
I really don't. But, however, I do know. I didn't drink. I didn't use. That's how.
That's what I know. That's how I know.
I say it because I can say it. But I don't want to risk my sobriety
by sounding like I'm bragging.

Near the end of 1995, I was coming from Switzerland,
an Italian part of Switzerland where Judy lived.
And I had sneaked drinking then.
Drinking wine. And you can't sneak drinking wine.
No way, man.

I was desperate to be sober.

So I was drunk on the airline flight back to Arizona. And got off the plane drunk as a skunk. You know what I mean.
And got busted by airport security for pissing against one of the poles that held up the airport entrance.

Why did you do it? That's what security asked me.
I said: Because I didn't want to piss in my pants and I don't know where the men's room is.
And I had to spend several hours in Tucson city jail.

Arguing like a drunk: "You can't throw a man in jail for being drunk."

"You can if the drunk is pissing on airport property."

I was desperate to be sober. Like I said. I wanted to be sober.

Police let me go after a few hours. And I walked all the way home
to 1st and Prince where I lived in a one room studio apartment.

I was sick for days. Despairingly sick. Hallucinating. Sick drunk.

Crawling on my knees and hands sick. Sick sick. Dying sick.

That's when I started running seriously. Barely able to walk, much less run. But I
did. Running for chrissakes? Running to save my life.

Yes, 1996. I should have known you then. Maybe I did.

I restarted outpatient therapy at Tucson VA hospital. Detox. Then therapy.
No-choice sessions. Mostly talking, mostly talking.
I'd take the city bus to the VA hospital. Until I started running there.
Impossible at first. I couldn't even do a mile first three tries.
A full six miles there. And six miles back.
Therapy buddies would say I was crazy to run six miles
in Tucson heat in the middle of the day.

Maybe I was crazy. Maybe so. Maybe? I was desperate to be sober.

And I started getting my teeth fixed at San Xavier IHS dental clinic.
At first I'd take the city bus with 2 changes to the dental clinic.
And then I started running there. 12 miles there. 12 miles back home.
I was really crazy then. I was sober though. And I drank lots of water.
Just about collapsed twice from the heat and dehydration.
But I had gotten back into decent shape. And I even got skinnier.

I should have known you then. Maybe I did. But I didn't know it.
I'd have asked you to run with me in the Rillito. Sandy trails for miles.

Some rocky places. Not fast running at all. Hot and dry miles. Miles of slow jogging. Exhausting. Don't know if you'd like it.

I was desperate to be sober. It was the only way I felt I could survive. So far, so good. With love. That's what got me through. I'll say that too. Love. And more love. And a lot of running in the hot desert of Arizona with love.

PICCOLO

Octave Higher Than the Ordinary Flute

FOR MY BROTHER PETUUCHE

many years ago when i was in the 8th grade
at Albuquerque Indian school i learned to play the clarinet
or tried to and did actually more or less and loved it   imagine me sitting on a
hard folding chair practicing and playing the clarinet

i didn't like practicing though   it was boring so boring
and some of the students looked like they were suffering or tortured   but i loved
learning the musical sounds and notes dancing dancing dancing and i loved the
gentleness and delicacy of our music teacher

later on in high school i played football instead of the clarinet
and little brother was in the school band and he played the clarinet and i would
listen to him practicing at home playing the clarinet   he'd close and lock the door
never wanting anyone to see him

he was funny about that   the music was the room he built around him and he was
inside it and would not come out until an hour later   and i'd stand outside his
locked door and i would dance to the music   funny ennit   one brother locked in
music and the other dancing

what a moment for an almost-80-years-ago memory   what a memory

RANDOM

Quite the figure.
More than.
Flare?
Flare pants.

I don't remember them well for some reason.
Yet I remember the move for some reason.
Memory is not notable for some reason.
As if there were no reason for a reason.

Thinking about you going to China for a long time.
Seems like a long time or feels like a long time.
Somehow unreal: A mental thing. Distance and time.

Like thinking. I used to read French writers mentally.
Since I don't know French, I read English translations.
Is that why I felt I could only comprehend French mentally?
Not emotionally or physically or spiritually but mentally.

I felt or figured that was the only way I could understand them.

Interesting. What does that have to do with flare? I don't know.

GRANDFATHER AND GRANDDAUGHTER

LISTENING AND HEARING

grandfather cuts a pear
with brown skin in half looks at it
and cuts one of the halves
and takes a little bite

sweet little bite and juicy

grandfather looks forward to lunch
with his oldest granddaughter krista
he wonders if she wonders about him
his age his work his breakfast his life

he looks at a good-sized dark red apple
and turns it over in his hand it is beautiful
with ripples of a hill undulating and a valley
he turns it in his hand and thinks

and brings the dark red apple to his nose
and sniffs and he smells when he was a boy
he walked to apple trees planted by his grandfather
near the river when he got to the trees he listened

to soft rushing sounds of the river through thickets
of willows and tamarisks and other tangles of brush
he can hear the sound of water flowing flowing
and a sweet bit of apple enters his remembering

he wonders if his granddaughter ever wonders
about him growing and growing with apple trees
by the river and he hears through tangles of brush
how clearly grandfather and granddaughter can hear

ALL OF THESE AND MORE LOVE

all of these
and more
and more
and more

Red Feather Woman's love and presence is.

This morning though my concern is Red Boy's. . .

sky dark gray in Beijing full
of questions unbounded unheeded
the hills blurred

going south is not the right direction
but what is anymore yet home
is there always waiting

red boy rises early and packs
baskets presents gifts holy sacred love
signs of his presence and journeys

the horizon is there though dark
still before the sun rises
he prays gentle now go east that way

and puts a prayer bag filled with cornmeal
into his shirt pocket and says they leave
with prayer good thoughts they go

REMINDER

I have a star quilt of my own now, different from yours.

This morning my mom said, 'I have these three quilts my grandmother made. Martha—my mom's aunt—gave them to me before she died.' My mom says she remembers her grandmother making the star pattern in quilts when she was growing up.

Makes sense to me. A star quilt. Of one's own.
Thomas and his Lakota wife lived in a two-story house
seven or eight prairie miles from Rosebud.

Prairie land all around. Of one's own.
Nothing and nobody but Lakota.

Prairie open to the sky. And the horizon without end.
Snow clouds. Storm clouds in March. And October.
Don't count blessings too soon. It will thunder and snow.
Thomas said, "Old man John Star Child said it. Once he saw
it hail big fist size balls of frozen snow. Thudding, thudding
down, thudding. It sounded like thunder on an August day."

Never make believe what you've seen, it's said. Twice
makes sense. A Tuesday, it was. Coming from Valentine,
we saw this cloud rise. Dark. Half a mile across. Swaying
like it was dancing. We could even hear a wind music like song.

There was an old house that looked like four hundred years
come and went. Nobody had figured what might have been.
Reminded me of a town that used to exist before gold came
to the people.

So they all went crazy looking for the stuff. Said it was the luckiest thing they
would ever have and know. So they went after it.

And the town eventually died.

JUMPING BEYOND

she jumps

aloft

into gray-black night

sky
moon

so so so so high

a silver disk

horizon cannot be anything less

than forever

jumping beyond is that

here   there

SONG

Heart beat song rain song and shuuti muuti all join in raining raining raining horizon to horizon mountain desert ocean joining in a song that cannot be denied.

Strong and gentle and firm assurance I feel that more than I've felt for a long time something new found but like it has been waiting for me to find it.

My morning run is not memory but fact within which my shoulders back hip leg feet mind spirit heart eye thinking feeling thrive and thrive in certainty.

In certitude really more than anything like breath is all it takes inhaling and exhaling mixing my breath with the breath of creosote cactus stone rain even asphalt.

No counting can be done for it is all part of a life we are carried by no segmenting or fracturing or saving for later on but breathing right now in continuation.

Like it is all necessary in sight of eye and mind and soul in touching and synchronizing endearment that is all that must be done not by necessity but choice.

Strangely I feel more certain of myself than I have felt for a long while and I am not questioning or doubtful about it but consider as organic and natural.

Normal and functional as rain in winter in the Phoenix valley brought about by powers beyond mere human effort but together with forces that can appear to be mystery.

Sometimes they are rightfully and quaintly so but purposeful and deliberate and right as rain no yes yes yes for that is what iatiku reminds us about when it rains.

Peh eh chah ah ah ah peh eh chah aneh eh kah aah chaaa ah breathing as inhale and exhale dancing with arms and hands up reaching to sky horizon and land horizon.

Ah neh eh kaachaa-ah ah limbs of leg and arm and hand weaving with spider grandmother's prayer song and story we know again to remember and to remember always.

Strangely though more than usual I feel happy healthy and wholesome words thoughts feelings of gratitude and love coming to me unbidden as offerings.

Duwah dah ah this here this way heh yah umaatse nieutra koodrumah eh nieuwoutrah skuwaahdruumah this way help will come to you and to all of us.

With the rain meeting the earth land and the earth land meeting the rain sparkling wetly gently like there are no restraints and physical limits at all.

Only a joining together with sound in voice and motion of body muscle and sentient provocation by prayer old women and old men hundreds and thousands of years ago singing.

Those still vibrant feral and fervent dawn running by not only me and shuuti muuti but in and with all things and all of everything as it was years and eons ago and still now is.

This morning's prayer is thank you to iatiku for accepting me as part of this ongoing life for air I breathe for earth land my feet tread and for the dawn light soon to come.

Accept me your child a boy and man a child and grandfather meant to not forsake the tremor of living that binds us to sacred life that needs nurturing from all of us.

Accept me once again this morning into the beauty before me and around me the sacred south mountain to my right and the holy and good desert to my left.

Please accept me as a component and element and questioner sometimes into your hand arm heart and vision so that I can always see and know I am one with all life.

Thank you for my poor song dance living and thriving. Thank you for my poor song dance living and thriving. Thank you for my poor song dance living and thriving. Thank you for my poor song dance living and thriving.

FLARING

Thought Into Color

red feather
into orange gold flaring
one moment real time
the next
a thousand and more years
beyond
as in returning
as in flying
into future story
as in present now
always flaring
gold orange
into feather red

PRAYERS FOR RAHO

THE NEXT 4 POEMS WERE WRITTEN OCTOBER 3, 2020 ARE FOR MY SON RAHO. THEY ARE ALL PRAYERS.

PAST

No one knows the past?

Yesterday was yesterday.
Last year was last year.
Yet we know we were born.

We were born from our mother.
And mother was born from her mother.
The past is always ours to know.

Yesterday and last year are yesterday and last year.
The truth of yesterday is always ours to know.

PRESENT

Here I am right now.
Here you are right now.
Step that way and I'll step this way.

Dance with me to this song.
This song shall be our present day.
Our present day will be our song.

Our song will be our present day.
Our present day will be our song.
Our present day. Our present song.

FUTURE

Some say the future is hard to know.
Good or bad or weird or just unknown or whatever.
Or unknown because we don't want to know.
Or it doesn't matter what the future is all about.

Caring is the best way to know the future.
It matters what we are doing now and tomorrow.
The future is what we have to care most for.
Good, bad, weird, whatever, unknown, we need to know.

CARING

I have a son who I love very much.
He's a grown man now but I remember him as a little boy.

He had heart surgery four days ago and now is in ICU still.
Tomorrow we will know more of his condition
and I do want to know and yet I also do not want to know.

I remember him at Canyon de Chelly as a little boy.
Running, hollering, laughing along the cliff edges.
A 3-year-old boy alive, unafraid, excited to be a child.
The sky so blue, the wind brisk, and me, a loving dad.

I love that memory of that boy, and I love him now.

Pray then. The past is past, it's yours. Pray then.
The present is yours; the past is now the present.
Future is tomorrow, and the next day after is future too.

Pray then. Pray then. Pray then. This prayer is yours.

HOW

is not to fear
but to question
without need
for need

hmmm wonder
is also need though
to ponder hmmm for
itself true or not

I don't know sometimes
and it's okay though some
will say, "but there are ways
to know" . . . yes true too true
but do we have to know
right that moment can't wait

climb hazard lava then
put your foot there then
on precipice that holds
now then turn dance
to tremor fragile so
light as dust mote with
air above and below
motion without quake

THUNDER FLOWER

shra'kaiyah is above diablo canyon

walking carefully down a steep stony and sandy trail
valley floor a mile and half away
on a hot afternoon after walking miles already
a sudden orange red flower stops me
suddenly in my tracks
                                    i don't know what it's called
orange red bright fire
stone walls above me are burnt
brown red and black
curving north and south
the mountain across the valley
fifteen miles away is black
pulling time distance close

fire bright red orange now here

A POEM THAT'S NOT A POEM BUT WHAT IT IS ONLY A POEM

CAN SAY WORDS AS SUCH ARE A POOR EXCUSE

FOR ANYTHING BUT A POEM

Hihdruutsi with love
Watching
Two young people
Before me
At a coffee shop table
Nuzzling and looking
At a pad of paper before them
I smile to myself
For their presence
And comfort and how happy they are
Or seem to be
The world is mighty
With fear trouble heartache
And such
But they don't mind or know
Or care

For now
Their moment is too precious
I write this
"this" with personal focus and bias

Then I look up
and they're gone
disappeared
were they there
ever
loving
innocent or innocence of a sort
and i'm still here
silent and sad with my question
were they there

O MY

o my
thank you o my
words rain upon
land
on my skin

o i can't speak
not words but breath
as wind
as song
as light

speak wind to me
we shall hear
we shall know
what there is
what our life is

o my o my a song
again i feel
must be the road
to forever mountain
in the midst
of always

love is more than a road
i remember my grandma
as a dark painful cry
difficult and hard to recall
but i must i must

A NEW DANCE SONG FOR THUNDER WOMAN

GENTLE AND STRONG

sing me song
dance me
dance you
                    a while
not long nor hard to do

slide and flow
dancing me
dancing you
                    a smile
song prance tune
turn twist too

more than a move
more than a hope
light light light we light

EAST IS SUNRISE. AND THEN WHAT?

with greetings always with love
speak to ooshrahtrah our father
light ask for forgiveness for mercy
so we may have strength and love

so love may be always in our words
always gentle strong presence for
ever with us mercy eh-meh heh-yah
enow'neeshru way to know ourselves

and how always we shall know ourselves
when violence and sheer lack of humility
are so fiercely thrown at us by those
shameless disgusting liars thieves killers

Shall we ask for mercy then?
For them? Or for us? Or for both?
And then what?

RED BOY THINKS, YOU THINK?

Red Boy thinks.
Spaced out is the way.
To be. Or not to be.
Make you come back.
Red Boy thinks. Smiles.
Wryly. Hmmm. Slyly too.

Shakespeare is nobody
but a writer and a poet.
So he's a well-known one.
One day at a time, AA says.
Doctor Bob, you know him?
Red Boy asks himself.
And says yeah and no.
So Shakespeare is well known.
So Red Boy is too, sort of. Maybe.

Any sonnet a day is good.
If you can write one, you're good.
Two is even better than good.
And three is: I don't know, maybe so.
Though sonnets are this and that way.
You know what I mean, don't you.
Red Boy shakes his head anyway.
He really doesn't know what the hey.
Sonnet, he thinks, go ahead and write.
And write some more until done.

Thou withers in the mirror.
Bright-eyed and clear-eyed at last.
Bright eyed and clear, clear, clear.
Like you see the end of the world.
20-20 vision, all is clear and concise.

Like made of glass, delicate and fragile.
Like the world isn't just any old day.
One day though who knows why.
Everything fell into pieces. Bright ones.
Clear broken glass, scatters of shatters.
In pieces. Don't cry, Red Boy, Red Boy.
Be happy and laugh no matter what.

GOING AND COMING

looking looking looking west
see you at a gas station stop
city or townscape roof horizon
that is nowhere but there
where you are is somewhere

looking looking looking west
see warrior woman drive
close enough to mountain top
that pushes at sky so blue
so blue it is forever all by itself

looking looking looking west
is distance but not far so far away
but is this side of sky where i am
blue blue my sky ai ai ai ai hey yaaa
now is everywhere like forever is now

looking looking looking west
i can see you everywhere you are now
tomorrow is another time to be yet
as highway skyway ridgeway snow way
ever so sky blue blue o my sky ai ai aiiiii

looking looking looking west
look this way to the next ridge so far
you can't see it yet but there you are
a being a woman a rider a carrier of song
the one warrior hummingbird women sing:

looking looking looking west
looking looking looking west
there to here here to there going going

looking looking looking west
looking looking looking west
here to there there to here coming coming

ODE TO A TREE, BY RB

Thou
is just a word

But tree
is never a shroud

But a crown
better suited

For mountain peak
as/or in to peak

As verb
not angst

For thou
art love ever

Singular and complete
and communal

As in ever
aren't thou?

Rb as in red boy

SCARES THE SHIT OUT OF ME

What happens now
Does it matter if we ask the question

Months ago i spoke with Pedro at Liberation Camp
He was alone at the camp

Where's everybody, i said
He smiled and said, taking a break
I thought ain't no time to take a break
The city is building building building freeway 202
Freeway is on the way, they ain't taking a break

Later i pictured me at a meeting and saying to Stephen,
O'odham tribal governor, i hear the tribe is helping standing rock, i hear it took
supplies up to the protest

To standing rock people opposing corporate development
Power power money money power power oil pipeline madness

Yeah, says governor Stephen, they need help

And i heard me saying, Pedro and others here need help too

Against phoenix freeway 202 power money and oil pipeline power money is aimed
at the hearts of Indigenous peoples and Their lands in arizona and north dakota

Ain't no time to take a break

> Sometimes Red Boy doesn't know what the hell to do. He feels like crying,
> but he doesn't cry even though he feels like crying. Sometimes, just
> sometimes though, he goes ahead and cries.

AWE

For Better Or Worse

pink flower tree
sky immense and more than the world
telephone & electronic wires above and below
no moment at all

sky is worldless and free
flower pink is now
wires are only wires
timeless as no need is

look again at sky
and find shadows below
a straight enough road close by
and too nearby on its sear way

we/i want sky to be our/my guide
an endless blue
minimalist and final a moment
as ever/never was and is and will not/be

KEE CUMEH SHEH DZAH'DZE HA'MAAH

DE'IEU-NAHMAA'TYUH. IT WAS BECAUSE ONE NEVER

APPRECIATED IT. KEE GUWAAH TSIEU-PEH-TAANIH?

HOW DID THE STORY GO?

Yellow Girl was crying with her head down
She was looking at the gray ground at her feet
She heard Grandma Kaa-maaskhuu say
Why are you sitting here crying

Koocheenih-naakuh kept crying loudly
with her sniffling boogers and tears falling
on her bare feet and onto the dry desert dirt
She cried, *Ooooooai* i can't get into the hole

Ooooaaaaieee ah-moomeh she hiccuped (loud)
I can't fit into that little hole she pointed shakily
at a little hole in the ground near a canyon cliff
So Grandma said, So sing with me sing with me

O Druuuh stheeeshuuu druuuh stheeeshuuu
Druuuh stheeeshuuu druuuh stheeeshuuu
Neetraa shkuuuhmah neetrah shkuuuhmah
Neetraa shkuuuhmah neetrah shkuuuhmah
But Grandma if I can't hide in the little hole
my husband will beat me again again and again
Aaiieee aaiieee aiyah Yellow Girl cried and cried
Looking at Skuuyuh Shruuwee coming to get her

Grandma said, Help me sing druuuh stheeeshuuu
a protection song *druuuh stheeeshuuu druuuh*
stheeshuuu druuuh stheeshuuu neetrah skuuuhmah
And soon Yellow Girl felt herself get smaller and littler
Until she was such a tiny size she could fit into the hole.

And when Skuuyuh Shruuwee, Monster Snake, could not
find her he roared *Ahwaaaooooooowah* and Koocheenih-
naakuh could hear him. And Grandma Spider heard him too

So remember: Grandma Spider helps you when you need help.
Make sure to thank her when she does. And, yes, you can depend on her.

I WAS THINKING OF TIME

Moment upon moment. Always time for time. You make me think and smile. I love that kind of silly thought moment.

Time and language and moment working together well when they happen. Like they do in story or as birds flying. Chirping as they suddenly fly away. No noise but chirps and flapping wings.

Dawaatra. That's moon's name in the Acoma language. Dawaatra. I don't know what it means exactly but it's what Acoma people call the moon.

I think it has something to do with parts joining together and/or becoming distinctive parts of each other.

Meaning of language is far-fetched at times though close enough in meaning and use.

Learning language is like breathing new breath in and out so our bodies are alive.

Good night, Dreams, I'll see you in my nights. Many So sang mournful sounds to me.

A quiet and tough source history is like marriage and love to understand.

If one can and will you understand when I get blue and feel hope is too hard to do?

Just words but a story. Just a story but words are the grace of it.

BUILDING AND HOLDING AND CARRYING

Worthy as sandstone heavy to pry or lift loose
from brown tan orange whitish layers in place
for countless thousands of years of ocean cover
years before humankind ever appeared one day
unknown as a weird stranger suddenly existent

Pondering confusedly already made in his own image
though he didn't get along that well with history
what ifs too present what ifs no use what's the use
if what-if thinking is so momentary and pointless
his image is familiar but causing too much disarray

Building with stone is learning from age and history
the man a stranger to stone when he cannot see time
as an agent not of memory but repetition layer on layer
brown tan orange white and ocean deep and deeper
mankind a question becomes too eager for answers

Sustain is not to maintain but to know resources
like stone is not final but it is helpful when all's gone
strength and willingness are gone useless as bragging
build by picking up stone laying it down caressingly
dancing while knowing that sustain is not to maintain

Busy as a bee is power shuffling 1-2-3 jump and flinch
friends visit and they bring cookies butter napkins jam
and puppies to smile and tell stories about doggy lives
once upon a time is good weather to laugh laugh upon
sustainability is possible and probably even fun somehow

Happy is nonsense so laugh and giggle and do not moan
that building and holding and carrying is great stuff true
sometimes the best reason not to cuss is because well . . .
because laughter is easy to lose but easy to get back again
when you're lucky to build hold carry even laughing works!

LOVE POEM CALLED QUITE A TASTY CAR, YEAH?

Quite a tasty looking car.

Luscious is its middle name. And last name too.

Yummmmeeeee is its asterisk.

Energeeee!

Is its power, not sugary icing.

Yummmeeee is its sign and punctuation too.

It's okay to eat in this car.

In fact, it's okay to eat this car.

Special made for a sort of flustered zen butterfly woman.

WONDER & HEAVEN-HELL

growing within christianity
is a risk
worth life and/or death
no choice then
when measure is not the point
but/and—is there
ever a time when life and life
are not so precious
and not i am not—
is not a real question or state
that just is there
query is an answer without a time
ask is an end
after all when there are no answers

when there are no answers and no questions
there is no strife or struggle nothing but ennui
moments unnoticed unnerving and unknown
without challenge or purpose then there's peace

purge of evil is pointless nor to celebrate victory

with this then
there is an odd quest for self
to not be
nor less or more but always true
and within

A LOVE POEM

Missing you.
See the sunset glow over the mountain.
Orange the sky a bit.
All that distance.

Just a photograph, one image.
Yet everything it means.
Present within.
All this time, all this way.

Love is an expression.
And a way for us.
To be present with each other.
It matters now.

Absence is for sure.
Notice, notice, and notice again.
Moment now and moment again.
Morrow is a wish. Morrow is presence.

So I send love again.
A pittance perhaps.
Such feelings there are.
It is all I have. Everything.

Is yours.
More than ever.
I feel fervor.
Love, love, and love again.

Ever is ever after all.
A moment I can stand.
A memory again.
Worthy. And more than that.

A poem of love?
Yes, and loneliness.
And longing.
Wish upon a star.

Again.
And again.
And again and again.
Ever ever and ever.

sjomehereinsantafenm

NEST

winging far far far
farther than distance
ever was a horizon

home a safe shade
warm and secure
so secure so known
a distance a place
more than anything else
and ever ever ever is

come then home
into here of no distance
a warm surety ever ever is

BEAUTIFUL

is more than word
is more than feeling
is more than thinking
is heart, bone, blood, hair, eye, nose
is soul, breath, physical act, and motion
is love and certainty that are now ours
is ours to have, hold, and keep
is to know and know more than ever
is to share with life life life with beauty
is the soul and real and solid and future that is

LOVE

Dawaa-eh always
within growth
an awareness of motion
our insight and outlook a horizon
sacred love shared
with all around always

with more love as resource
and foreground and container
always to be taken care of

GUWAADZI, AMOO-UH

sky mountains
clouds deserts
night moments
star murmurs

language is ours
no matter how mute
voice and words are
we are life life life true

with love we are
with place and time
with day and night
murmuring forever now

REPETITION

i can only repeat love i love you

more more and more

from here deserts and mountains and oceans are forever like stars

more more and more

all around all deep into the night and day beyond time

more more and more

from there where stars are forever we are deserts mountains oceans

they repeat us we repeat them

a continuum of repetition is our existence

a continuum of repetition is their existence

deep into day and night beyond time

deep into night and day beyond time

SPOONFUL CAN HAVE AND SHOULD HAVE TWO L'S?

Sebastiano and his boy's tiny feet drumming
Softly across the desert gently.

Kaiya and her little girl's words rich and richer
With discovery and knowledge.

We need such drumming.
We need discovery and knowledge.

And we are lucky to know children
Like Kaiya and Sebastiano.

Again and again and again, they show us love, light, vision.
Growing, laughing, discovering, knowing.

SHARING. BREATHING. TALKING. LOVING YOURSELF.

LOVING OTHERS.

Talking. Speaking. Crying. Sometimes crying is not enough. Even talking is
sometimes not enough. Loneliness is being alone in cruel pain and hunger.

Listening to others. To each other. Hearing someone tell you of her or his
pain is sharing. Sharing pain is better than lonely pain. Aching alone is torture.
Crying and cursing alone is not very cool at all. Suffering by yourself is
self-torture. Drinking by yourself is too. Who needs that? Not me. Not you.

Not your wino buddies. Drinking alone is too easy. Drinking with others
is not so cool either. Laughing at your mistakes, calling yourself a weak ass!
That's your excuse for losing your last job. Misery is more misery—that's truth.

Misery is your middle name? You laugh when you say so. But it's not funny.
Remember they used to call you Microscope in high school at AIS? Yeah, they did.
Because you were going to go to college to become a chemist, remember?
You started college with that plan but didn't go on because of the "prejudice"!
You said white students got more attention than Indians. And they were favored.
By professors, you said. Bias against Skins! So that's why you quit college.

So your hurt is deep inside. Within heart, blood, liver. And in your face scars,
knife cuts on your hands and face. So you cry about it when you tell stories
that are funny and goofy. But sad too. Loser: that's what they call you. A name
you hate and rage. It's not only colonialism or racism or race prejudice, man,
It's yourself who has spread the lie to yourself for your lack of self-respect.

Anger and fear. Cursing yourself as a loser. Damn me, fuck it all, hellfire, you say.
I've heard you shout and scream: I don't know what to do but curse this insanity.
The angry, scary, hateful way makes no sense at all. Curses-hatred-fear is more
senseless nonsense and isn't the way. Misery isn't your middle name. Then sing:
Misery isn't my middle name. Try that out. Call yourself a winner, man. A true life.

FLOURISH

Flourish

        Flourish   Flourish

      Flourish   Flourish   Flourish

Flourish   Flourish   Flourish

Flourish

Yes yes yes just like flourishing in California in late winter

FLOURISH!

Hi Jami Love,

I go ahead and say aloud the above as I type it out.

It feels good. Gentle, quiet, breathing sound. Makes me feel relaxed. Relaxing sound. Hi Jami Love. Guwaadze Jami ahmoo-uh. A relaxed breathing sound.

Love that feeling of gentle, good relaxed breathing when I say and hear the sounds of the words.

Language is at the base and core of relating to others. Language is motion. Action. Doing. Letting. Sharing. Being active with sounds of communication. Touching. I think I want to be a poet in the use of language. That's the true nature of poetry I believe. When it is in power gear, you can feel the action of it. Holding. Sharing. Word and sound holding. Holding us.

I love you. Amoo . . . shrowtseemuh . . . I love you. Simple. Direct.

When I walked into our Ahwatukee home, I stopped at the door and prayed with corn meal. Yes, I did. Because I found my little buckskin cornmeal bag yesterday. I was so happy. It was on my desk here at the condo. Found it—or it found me— when I was clearing stuff off my desk.

My prayer was simple: Thank you. Thank you, Staishtahnee, for returning to me. I missed you very much. I love you. I was lost a minute or two about it but I'm okay now. Thanking you again again again. Yes, for finding me too.

Or words to that effect. Hmmmm. Yeah, I was very happy this morning I was able to pray with s'kaahdeenah before I entered inside, saying, Guwaadze Kqaiyah, Hihdruutsi nieu-puguuh. Hihdruutsi is entering. Thank you, Grandmothers and Grandfathers, speaking on behalf of my beloved Jami and me. Thank you. We send our Words-Breaths into Creation-World-Life all around us.

And sent our Words-Breath into Creation-World-Life all around us.

EVER

Like Air
Like Sky
Like Land
Like Ocean
Like Love
Like Life

Words are words
We are to make work
From concept to act
Nothing in between ever

Poetry is the same
Have it mean what we say
First time second time
And ever after is poetry

THANK YOU

Forever is too meager as a word

A mere word made of letters or script

When life is a world of wonder and awe

Wherein we thrive as meager script within wonder and love

LETTER FROM INDIO

Dear Mom and family,

On my way to Tacoma, now 2 days of travel by bus,
I am in Indio, California. Monday and Tuesday have passed.
And one more day or so until I arrive at my first job

It is dry desert here with desert mountains nearby. Indio.
Bus travel is tiring. But don't worry, I am young and strong.
Here I sit at a small table in the bus depot cafe with others.

I hope all of you are well, especially my little brothers and sisters.
Growing and growing all the time. Dear Mom, I wish you all well.
Indio is somewhere in the middle of nowhere or everywhere.

I miss you all, I have to say. I think of all of you. But I am fine.
Leaving home yesterday, walking to the highway, that was hard.
But today after riding the bus all day and all night, all is better.

I will work hard. Training as a nurse, now to be working as a nurse.
That is what I am looking forward to. Please don't worry about me.
With your love and my kuumeh, my courage, I will always be safe.

On the bus depot wall, a sign says WELCOME TO INDIO. Just that.
Welcome to Washington. Maybe there will be a sign like that there.
Please be strong, healthy, and happy. I send love, Daughter, Rachel.

We pass through, then we pass through again.

YEARS OF PAST, PRESENT, FUTURE. MEMORY. TOWARD LOVE.

FOR ZANIAH, GREAT-GRANDDAUGHTER

Years of pain, years of pain. Feelings and feelings do not recede.

We recede though, even disappear. Never to be seen, except by ourselves.

Before anything else, we go away. Hide. Hoping to never be visible.

Years, years, years of fear, anger, careless and careful to a fault.

We keep the pain hidden in plain sight. Memory is easy. Never lost.

Moment by moment, instance by instance, question by self-question.

Walking: I learned to walk, although I do not recall how I learned.

I watch my great-granddaughter walk bravely, confidently, happily.

WANTING AND NEEDING

Wanting

And needing
Breath
Breath
And breath again
Assurance and reassurance
That is there
For us to breathe and breathe ever
As love nourishes us
Again and again

Repeating and refreshing
Assuring and reassuring
Life and life and love and love
and again again and again again

I love you
And I love you
Again again and again again

HUMMINGBIRD HUMMING

Early morning then.
Time is no difference. No matter.
No consequence. When time is timeless.
I wish it were 5:59 AM again though.
Just to know it's possible.
Mei Mei was happy to see me.
Yes happy as her dog eyes say.
I smile.
Yes, happily, I smile.

Hummingbird is wishing.
I think I feel I sense I am me.
Hmmmmm. I think I feel I sense I am.
Did you ever think of how thinking started?
I just did and I had to answer I don't know.
And, yes, that must be the way thinking started.
Hummingbird is wishing.
I am happy to be back in Santa Fe.
Unquestionably happy to be here.
Odd, isn't it. I'm a kid in his 70s happy with aging.
That's kinda startling but it also feels okay.

Mei Mei and I are going to walk a bit now.
For her constitutional needs. Or is it called "pp needs"?
Whatever it is, it's necessary and an actual fact.
See you later. Talk to you later.
By the way, this is not a poem, just informal casual writing.

And also I love you and more on a Saturday morning.

light strands between shells and cactus

To be alive is to be between.
As between within breath and no breath.
Sky above and the land below.
Water in rivers and oceans and oceans and deserts.

Between is to be nurtured
By hummingbirds and crows.
By wind and oxygen and sunlight.
By now and never before like this.

Light is our source from a star.
We're the in-between star and soul.
Movement in lung and blood red
Morning breeze and stony hill slope.

Right now, thinking of love and you.
Yours and mine, what's in between.
Moment is forever and the past.
Love then is to live through and by.

Love within, then love.
Love all around, love on.
Love above us, ever love.
Love below us, always love.

LOVE IS NOW AND NOT TOO SOON NOR TOO LATE

A moment before is not too soon.

A moment later is not too late.

Now now.
Love is now.
As in now is love.
Love ever is ever.

"When you're old, I will change your diaper," she says.
Driving the car, he smiles and nods. And he thinks again.

When I turn 110 you will be 77 years old, he says silently.
Time and age go on and on and on and on and on, ever.

Rarely does a boy know enough to know he will grow old.

Ever is now a moment from now, not too soon nor too late.

FLOWERING

Don't forget, she said as they turned to leave. She turned her head to face the water falling and flowing from the sandstone ledge into a little pool of bright water. He watched her head and face swivel to the thin clear rivulets of spring water flowing down the stone canyon wall. Her eyes glistening, her voice lightly trilling. Something whirling in the soundless air around them. Within Yeownee Canyon, shrub juniper, cactus and yucca and wild onion, sandstone debris cluttering steep canyon slopes nearby.

I'll never forget, he said. 10 years, 20 years, 40 and 50 years pass. If one should go back to Tse'tsee Ais'shtyuu Gumuustah, she or he will know the passing and going on of a timeless time, the soundless air whirling around in the canyon. And the experience, sensation, feeling, change, history, happiness, sadness, disappointment, the great joy, the gamut of human struggle and event. And the love we shall always know and share.

SHE WRITES A POEM WITH LOVE. I WRITE A POEM WITH LOVE.

She writes: thank you for your
letter and for you. for all that
you are and for the boy-man
aanyu'meh human being you
are. i love you.

So with happiness, i write:

leap
into sky
dig into
ground
being human
is to be a link
between
sky
and
ground
and
life.

LOOKING FORWARD

Look forward to go forward, you must.
Yaanee nuwaakahmeh-eh kudruu-stah, shteh-gaadzeh.

We have to look forward when we are to move forward.
Yaanee nuwaakahmeh-eh kudruu-stah dzee yaanee nudeh-ehku shruustah-tyahnuh.

We have to look forward if we are to move forward.
Steh-gaazeh yaanee new-kachaanah shruustah dzee yaanee nuudeh-ukuu
shruustah-tyanoh.

Mahatma Gandhi looked forward.
Mahatma Gandhi choo-uuh'kaah yaanee.

India has always been itself: land and people!
India tuu-dyuu truushraah dzah: haatse eh hanoh.

India has always been itself.
India tuu-dyuu truushraah dzah!

PARENT - CHILD - REPLY

Love calls
Desert hears
Dusk lights

Ever returning
Breath
Life & life & life & on & on

Daughter is
Father is
Desert dusk life on and on

Children we are
Unknowing as ever
So we can abandon loss

Rainy at twenty-one
A daughter forever
A child forever

Me at fifty-three
A father forever
A child forever

A gift and happiness
A wonder
Family family ours yours

Yours and ours forever
Within and without
Sphere and sphere

Love binds our lives together when we let family and families grow. And we grow
with love.

THERE AND EVER

A China Moment

Mountains and prairies and forever
Count and count and count to no end
Time distance parts pieces ever ever
Space is spare after all kinds of common

There is there is there and everywhere

Rivers are running rushing roaring
Loudly from mountains to lands lands
And also lovely softly musically gently
Lively praying whispery sighing songs

Everyone is there with everyone everywhere

Water from Himalayas' highest peaks now
Magic as brilliant crystal truth more
Than what we expect to wash with or drink
There is liquid lasting eons in a bright flash

Time is not measurable and forever is ever

Qinghai is memorable but only vastly for now
Sight line is too slow to be captured now
What we need is escape but not to flee now
Holy land as ever shall be ever sacred now

We see without sight but sight is ours always

Thou will not forget ever mountains and prairies
Always China is everywhere we need to be
A sight final and quickly we must be there so
Too we can be there in that you are there now

QCUI'SKAH KAHGUUTRUTIH, AMOO-UH ALWAYS

Yes, we have grown together. And kept growing.
Over time. Years, months, weeks, days, minutes.
Time as motion for us. Always in motion.
We have grown within each other.
More than we realize I believe.
And we have come to believe more in life.

Love has been key in all ways.
Even in painful and hurting ways.
With you, with me, we have lived love.

Always in motion, morning, day, night.
Love is demanding love we believe.
And more love is the result and unending.

The work-art we do has grown with love too.
It shapes us as we grow with our art-work.
We must let it form us as it must and will.

Qcui'skah Kahguutrutih and Hihdruutsi.
Two people loving each other, sharing, holding.
Held secure by love gently, happily, eagerly, always.

ALL BEST, SIMON J. ORTIZ

I sign my letters
With "All Best" and then I write my name.

Simple as love.
Simple as I can see and say
as I can see and say it.

From the me I know.
An Indigenous man within the USA nation.

Who disagrees with the USA
As the most warlike nation I have ever known

That has waged war and more war
Upon Indigenous peoples from the very beginning to now.

War. I plead and curse against war now
and forever and for the war to cease and for love to surge.

Love yes, love yes, love now.
And forever pain, death, loss to stop forever now. Now.

So me and my peoples and all peoples will be safe.
And be safe, secure, and able to write "all best" as they love and live.

Yes, love, love, love
For our children, our families, friends, lands, dogs and cats, with more love and
more love.

FACE TIME FACE

face time
is goodness

love
gentleness

face touching
with loving fingers

eyes loving
gentle roving

face time
is within

and outward
as love

breathe then in
and out like love

goodness gentleness
aliveness awareness

ours to have and hold
ours always and more

life of love
love of life

ours as love for all
love as ours for all

After my run this morning,

I came to you when you called me,
and we talked gently and I loved you for wanting a hug
and a kiss and another kiss on your cheek.

After a period of quiet and you went back to sleep,
I watched you as I lay beside you: love now always
a gentleness, a quiet morning with the good sun,
so alive, you are so gently asleep; so much love.

What a feeling is I don't really know but it is gentle
most times and I feel its quietness joining me.
Sometimes for some reason I try to slip away unseen
but I don't manage to do it; I stay and love and love.

What is feeling anyway if you can't be enclosed by it
and drawn into calm and peace and a good quiet.
That's what and when it matters, entering the space
made by your feeling so you can stop and know it.

Don't forget to look at the moon and the mountains.

Silvery white platter
In purple blue-black darkness
Deep forever.
A moment and place called infinity.

Stop everything somewhere in the mountains
And say memory is everything.
Do not forget a thing
For a million years and more.

Mountains and the moon is a name.
To keep
And to be kept by your side ever
No matter what you lose or gain.

Don't forget to sing; don't forget to pray breathing.
This moment is now love; this moment is now love.
Love is this moment now; love is this moment now.
Moment love is this now; love is this moment now.

VALENTINE'S DAY, FEBRUARY 2022, LOVE IS STILL LOVE AND MORE

Outside the window, the big cedar tree still stands
tall and taller ever.
Let the ache alone; let it be itself,
an ache.
Love ever, instead.

Always a recall, any time lacks more than enough.
Daytime nighttime or no time.
I'm still ever here. Even when I move closer.
Or closer and/or even closer.

With you, a Valentine is a Valentine, no matter what.
Or where or why or how. Because love is love and more love.
Ever and forever.
Yours I am with the cedar tree as big as ever. And more love.

WAY TO GO, DYLAN

Jazz on the sax is a journey.

Into and within the song.
Song will take you there.

Where there is there.
Where song is there.

A power to reckon by oneself.
To be reckoned with in music.

A way of going. Going forward.
Knowing the way to go. Forward.

With the song.
Into the song.
Within the song.

Heart, head, soul,
Spirit there there.
Where there is there.

WE SHALL ENDURE

March 1973. Forever. Always. Never-ending. Continuing.

It was snowing in the Southwest, and the wind was cold and harsh the past few days.

We know better than to think it'll be like this forever. No way.

FBI, US marshals, and BIA police in full battle gear surrounded Indigenous Peoples at Wounded Knee.

Again, we know better than to feel it'll be like this always.

Then the Gallup city police shot and killed Larry Casuse.

Resist then—let them know resistance is never ending.

Police shot, shot, shot. A Navajo Vietnam vet was down the street.
He heard the firing. He cried, "I was at Khe Sahn. I was at Khe Sahn."

Continuing. To live, grow, love, have family, take care of the land. Yes, always continuing. Continuing.

CASUSE

As a UNM student leader, Larry Casuse encouraged others
to be active on behalf of Indigenous matters and peoples.

When Emmett Garcia was named to the Board of Regents for University of New
Mexico, Casuse called him a "false person."

Garcia owned Navajo Inn, a bar of the worst sort, where Navajos and others were
trapped by alcohol use and sales. Due to its location on a main Navajo road to and
from the rez, many fatalities and injuries took place there.

Garcia was presently the Mayor of Gallup, a New Mexico border town. At
the same time, Garcia was also head of the Gallup-McKinley County Alcohol
Rehabilitation Program.

One hand feeding the other hand. Busy. Profiting. Busy, yes.

Those were only a few of the reasons why Casuse opposed Garcia as a UNM Board
of Regents member.

There was also the reason why Indigenous peoples opposed Gallup Indian
Ceremonial that took place annually. Profiting.

Gallup Independent, a local newspaper, reported Casuse abducted Garcia in order to
march him around the state. To educate him. Would Garcia have learned anything?

With a small firearm, Casuse and Bob Nakaidinae forced Garcia to march with
them down a street to a sporting goods store.

Police had been alerted. Larry and Bob waited. And waited. At the store.
When police arrived, they ordered Casuse and Bob to come out.
After Casuse and Bob unclothed themselves, they began to exit. Bob was first, and
he was arrested.
When Casuse exited the store, police began shooting and shooting. Casuse was killed.
Very dead.

RESISTANCE

I am an alcoholic, a non-using alcoholic since I stopped drinking in winter of 1995,
So I know the devastation of it.

I know the cause of death by it too, and I am able to say I didn't die.
Or go crazy or end up in jail forever. I am alive. Alive for real.

We have to resist, no matter what. To stop fighting what is wrong
is death. We have to live in order to live. To live is to matter.

We have to stop people like Emmett Garcia who are harmful.
And we have to stop ourselves when we are also destructive.

Resistance is necessary when we decide to make a stand.
To make a stand for life is to live in order to live. To not die.

When young Indigenous leader Casuse opposed Garcia,
he was making a stand for the lives of Indigenous peoples.

To resist by making a stand for life cost Casuse his own life.
Unfortunate for society and its police carrying out NM's wrath.

Resistance is necessary to correct what's wrong. Believe me.
We must live in order to live. It matters to live. And to die.

MARCHING

Being There Alive

Three weeks after Casuse was killed, a memorial march was held in Gallup; it was also billed as ongoing support for Wounded Knee.

The 1973 AIM occupation of Wounded Knee, South Dakota, site of a massacre in 1873 where hundreds of Lakota—women, men, children—were killed by US cavalry was currently going on.

Before the Gallup march began, Toledo, a Jemez Pueblo elder, spoke to the massive crowd of people. He said, "We must act with dignity." Several times, he said that. That was his message. "The People must act with dignity." There is strength in that. To show our courage by having dignity. To act with dignity.

The People cheered and shouted for Toledo's good words:

"We must act as who we are as human persons. Don't let anyone provoke you to violence. We are strong People."

A telegraph from Wounded Knee was read aloud. From the sisters and brothers who were there: "We are remembering our brother Casuse. We're fighting for the same things he fought for and gave his life for."

One of our other march leaders spoke. "We are here for all humanity, for that purpose. We are here to let Gallup know, to let New Mexico know." To remember Larry Casuse, our brother, to not let his effort and passing on be in vain.

There was a huge swell and surge of hollering, piercing whistling, cheering, keening—from our growing numbers of peoples—Black, White, Mixed, all races and ethnicities of peoples in the Americas and beyond—and countless Indigenous tribal peoples and communities on the march. We must live in order to live.

MUST

We must live and decide for ourselves what our lives are to be. Each and every year, each day, each minute of our time on Earth matters.

We must believe in what we are doing. We must be sure of what we are doing in order to survive and be sustainable and go on and on and on.

We must be sure of what we are doing as we live.

We must be certain of what kind of life we are to live within.

We must be sure to value the past, present, and the future.

We must respect, honor, and help others always and always.

We must believe in love because without love nothing is possible.

Must is a word that has to do with responsibility, obligation, humility, simplicity, gratitude, integrity.

Must is also a word having to do with respect, honesty, fairness, equality, and reliability.

And must also means: we must allow ourselves to live.

CLEAR CREEK

A Favorite Love Poem?

there there where where
where miasma is
akin to
direction like there where
knowledge and more knowledge reside
where where there there

forget and remember three words
up down there within memory
but which is where sense is lost
it doesn't matter does it
miasma is the doing and undoing
knowledge when i was a boy
was possible and impossible
to understand

hmmmmm you know
in english acquumeh niah then tehneh niah
say again hmmmmm

throws into balance with unbalance
after all
english is like acquumeh after all
after all that thinking about possibility
and impossibility

yes i'd love to go back to clear creek
beautiful like you say so beautiful
you are when you tell me to love you

POETRY IS LIKE THIS

Forever Life With Words

Water

Air

Dirt

Tumble weed

Are words we need

Drink drink so your blood flows on and on and on
So sweat feels wet on skin down your neck and arm
So sand glistens when sunlight slants on surface
A small small small plant begins as herbal trembling
Earth as land needs space and horizon needs wording

Running makes you breathe hard and fast
Sex also makes you huff and puff and huff and puff
We see through space clear and far and certain
Imagine yourself a plant's bud turning into flower
That never ends like air is there holding and holding

Dirt is dirt is dirt nevertheless it is our cradle
Miracle is otherwise cross the bridge first
Then ask if you made it by accident or by plan
And go ahead again and say dirt is dirt is dirt
Gratitude starts at dirt bottom believe it as truth

Spring begins growth at winter's tumultuous end
With seed of a tumbly tumbleweed i've never seen
Earth is free after all even though we doubt miracles

A moment ago is never too late a little leaf of life lives
Behold wonder at how we accept breath nevertheless

Yes, water we need need need and need we need too
Yes, air we need like story true or not air as truth so
Yes, dirt is just dirt dirty as dirt untruth dirt needed too
Yes, so we can grow tumbleweeds sing so we grow and go
Yes, words words words words words forever life with words

HOW AND WHY AND NOT KNOWING

Is not to hear
But to question
Without need
For need

Hmmm wonder
Is also need though
Ponder hmmm for
Itself true or not

I don't know sometimes
And it's okay though some
Will say but there are ways
To know. . . . yes true too true
But do we have to know
Right that moment can't wait

Climb the jagged lava then
Put your feet there
The precipice will hold
Now then turn dance
To tremor fragile so
Light as dust mote with
Air above and below
Motion without quake
And with.

I THINK YOU WOULD HAVE LOVED ME WHEN I WAS A BOY

Many many years ago
Well actually almost 80 years ago now

That's not too long ago
Is it

And you would have loved the little river—chuu'nah
We all called it—as it was then
Winding and curving slow in places and fast other places
I loved every bit of it yeah every bit

Cottonwoods and willows and reeds and bushes
To play amidst them and the sunlight and shadows too
And fun and we would take our small herd of sheep
That way sometimes with our cousins

Like heeshah'meeh who we knew then as melford
Yeah the same melford who actually spells it m-i-l-f-o-r-d
I didn't know that until last year when he persisted
To be the head of his family when his sister actually was

Oh well that's him by training and work as a surveyor

Being a kid playing alongside a beautiful little river was good

The river was where the goats lived and were wild
Although actually they were domestic goats that became wild

Runaway goats

Domestic farm goats turned wild
You know what i mean
Tame farm goats turned into wily wild ones

Skinny, fast, feisty, ornery and smart ass goats!
You should have seen them
Bright eyes, yeah, sparkly eyes looking at you side ways

Watching your every move yeah that kind of look

Free like kids
Free like Red Boy
They would watch us kids
Playing war or fishing or hassling each other

Yeah you would or might have loved me as a boy kid

sjo/12-16-17, a kid bright and sparkle-eyed

THE END

Any sonnet a day is better than good.
So if you can write one, you're good.
Two is even better or gooder than gooder.
And three is: I don't know maybe so.
Though sonnets are this and that way.
You know what I mean, don't you know?
Red Boy nods his head any way anyway.
But he really doesn't know what the hey.
Sonnet, he thinks, go ahead and write.
And write some more until done gooder!

ACKNOWLEDGMENTS

THANK YOU to the editors of the following journals and anthologies in which earlier versions of some of these poems appeared: *World Literature Today, Red Ink International Journal, Monticello in My Mind: Fifty Contemporary Poems on Jefferson, Amaravati Poetic Prism, Hai Shi Journal,* and *Poetic Olives of August: Sino-American Poetic Sharing.*

Thank you to the Mesa Refuge for my 2019 residency as a Full Circle Indigenous Writers Fellow.

Thank you to Amerind Museum for hosting events I was a part of, including recitation of works included in my books.

Thank you to University of Arizona Press for its outstanding support of Indigenous literature and its many, many readers.

Thank you to Henry Oso Quintero, James Blasingame, Kenny Redner, Ruben Cuc Bac, and Paris Masek for their friendship and loyalty. And thank you to Tyson Powless, Dushawn John, and Laura Tohe who were associated with *RED INK International Journal* at Arizona State University.

Thank you to my beloved partner, family, and friends for their enthusiasm and support of my writing.

Thank you to Chen Si'an for translating some of these poems into Chinese.

Thank you to Arizona State University, San Francisco State University, University of Arizona, University of Oklahoma, Northern Arizona University, Beijing Normal University International Writing Center, and the literary festival and event organizers in Sells, Arizona, China, India, South Africa, and Eswatini for inviting me to read my work at communal events in their regions during the time I was working on these poems.

NOTES

A SORT OF POEM OR SORT OF STORY FOR RED PETAL GIRL

Red Petal Girl, the name that appears in this poem and others, is a name created by Jami Proctor Xu and used in her letters, as well as her poem, "field of ten thousand flowers," published in her chapbook, *Hummingbird Ignites a Star*, and in her Chinese poetry collection, *Turan Qiwu (Suddenly Starting to Dance)*.

HOW DID YOU KNOW I WOULD BE HERE I DON'T KNOW I SAID
I JUST DID

The title of the poem is a line from Jami Proctor Xu's poem, "corn poppy."

QUAILS CAME BY AND MADE ME SMILE. THEY MAKE ME LAUGH THE
WAY THEY'RE ALWAYS TALKING AND PLANNING WHAT TO DO.

The title of the poem is from a line in an email from Jami Proctor Xu.

FREEDOM AND THE LIE: MONTICELLO AND THOMAS JEFFERSON
AND THE PLAN

This poem is a revision of a poem I wrote in collaboration with Jami Proctor Xu several years ago.

TURNING

This poem is written after Jami Proctor Xu's poem, "Zither," published in her Chinese collection, *Turan Qiwu (Suddenly Starting to Dance)*.

CRYSTAL. CHRYSTALS.

The passage, "I think another thing about life that's a huge gift is that it's possible to go back. To take oneself back to a place of pain at a later date, when you are both the same person and a different person," is by Jami Proctor Xu. It is from one of her email communiques to me. Ideas, moods, reminders are inspirational and crucial. Ideas, moods, reminders are inspirational and crucial.

THAT GIRL

The following lines are quoted from an email by Jami Proctor Xu:

"As a girl. . . . Crumbled in my palms" squatting or sitting or crouching "by a pond."

"walked across the grass and the feather ball waited there, soft-soft."

"As a girl, sometimes I sat on the dried mud by a pond, picking up pieces of dried mud. Flat shapes made when earth cracks itself. Sometimes the pieces crumbled in my palms, sometimes I lifted a small corner and a whole piece came, solid, together, still wet on the underside. Dirt belly. It made me smile. Sometimes I rubbed the mud on my own skin."

"Just after I swam. And thought of Ceremony having saved my life so many times. I came up for air and hummingbird flew right over my head. After weeks of not coming. Then I got out of the pool, walked across the grass, and the feather ball waited there. Soft-soft."

"lifted a small corner and a whole piece came, solid, together, still wet on the underside, dirt belly."

Connections have to do centrally with ageless oral tradition via today's electronic life lines of communication. Life and its wonders waited for Jami, as it did for Nautsiti.

WHAT IS THE SHAPE OF A LEAF?

The poem title is from Jami Proctor Xu's poem, "density of green, chengdu." My poem was written as a response to her poem.

DREAMS AND REALITY

The beginning of the poem "Dreams and Reality" refers to the Qing Dynasty Chinese novel, *Dream of the Red Chamber.* Tradition erases, in a sense, the line between cultures. In a sense, we, as distinct peoples, are cultural allies, not opposites.

SALVATION OR ELSE
The following passage is quoted from an email from Jami Proctor Xu:

"in 1996, when shery died, there was a severe drought in tucson. we'd all been waiting and waiting for the rain. you could see things starting to die. less baby animals that spring. i remember after she died, i prayed for rain, prayed and prayed and prayed for it. i felt like i was going to die if it didn't come. and after a few days, it did come. i ran outside barefoot. walked over the gravel in my parents' driveway, letting the rain soak me. the raindrops merging with my tears. two doves flew past me then. i always remember those doves.

that rain.

i knew i would be able to make it then."

REMINDER
The following lines quoted from an email by Jami Proctor Xu:

"I have a star quilt of my own now, different from yours. This morning my mom said, 'I have these three quilts my grandmother made. Martha—my mom's aunt—gave them to me before she died.' My mom says she remembers her grandmother making the star pattern in quilts when she was growing up."

SPOONFUL CAN HAVE AND SHOULD HAVE TWO L'S?
The title of this poem is taken from Jami Proctor Xu's line in an email, "I think spoonful should have two L's."

LIGHT STRANDS BETWEEN SHELLS AND CACTUS
The title is a line from an email from Jami Proctor Xu.

ABOUT THE AUTHOR

SIMON J. ORTIZ is a retired Regents Professor from Arizona State University, so he's no longer active faculty who teaches. Yet he still finds himself teaching through the poetry, short fiction, and essays that he writes.